Katherine,
Congratulations!

David McCroskey

THE BEST DAY OF YOUR LIFE

CONQUERING ADVERSITY
THROUGH
ACCEPTANCE, ATTITUDE, AND ACTION

BY DAVE MCCROSKEY

"When I die, I want someone to thank God that I lived."

THE
BEST DAY
OF
YOUR
LIFE

CONQUERING ADVERSITY
THROUGH ACCEPTANCE,
ATTITUDE, AND ACTION

BY DAVE MCCROSKEY
FOREWORD BY DR. JACK SCHAAP

First Printing – July 2011
Second Printing – March 2012

ISBN: 978-0-9845961-3-3

All Scripture quotations are from the King James Bible.

CREDITS
Cover Design: Suzanna Cranston
Page Design and Layout: Linda Stubblefield
Proofreaders: Rena Fish and Linda Stubblefield

To order additional copies of this book, please contact
Dave McCroskey
3574 Pelzer Avenue
Montgomery, AL 36109
(334) 318-5641
davemccroskey@gmail.com

Printed in the United States of America

DEDICATION

To My Parents: Rodney & Lori McCroskey

Thank you for loving blindly, suffering immeasurably, and sacrificing completely. Thank you for always believing in me and telling me that I could do anything that I ever wanted to do. You mean more than you'll ever know and more than I could ever try to express. I owe you everything. I love you so much.

Your Son

ACKNOWLEDGMENTS

I was very selective in who I listed in the acknowledgement section of this book. Many hundreds of people have made a difference in my life and either directly or indirectly allowed this project to come to fruition. For the sake of brevity, however, these are the people who directly made my dream come true and have made me the person I am today. Thank you all—you will never know what you mean to me.

MY SAVIOUR

You've given me so much. You gave me a Christian family, wonderful people, and a home in Heaven. I love you and long to serve you with my life!

THE FAMILY

Angela McCroskey: I could have never written a book without a big sister who taught me how to write my name. I love you, Angela. You're the best.

Kimberly McCroskey: My buddy. You are so much fun, so bright, so vibrant, and so sweet. We will always be best friends.

Joshua McCroskey: You're the man! Thanks for putting up with me and for being such an awesome roommate. Thanks for letting me keep the light on into the wee hours of the night while I wrote this book. I love and admire you.

THE GANG

Daniel Kokubun: We have cried, prayed, and philosophized late into many a night. You are a big part of who I am. Thanks for "getting it."

Derrick Sandridge: You challenge me to be a better man, Christian, and friend. There are so many attributes that you possess that I long to emulate. Let's tear it up for Him!

Preston Vaprezsan: We have truly lived, laughed, loved, and learned—and we've done it all together. I will always "Remember the Name." I am David; you are Jonathan. I love you, Preston.

Johanna Forster: God has been very kind to bring you into my life. You're an amazing and incredible lady. I can't wait to see how God uses your life…it's going to be special!

Emily Hamilton: You understand that life is too short to be average. Thank you for changing my life—now go change the world.

God has brought so many wonderful friends into my life. Time would not permit me to list them all…but here are the best of the best. I love you all so much. You make life worth living in so many ways. Derek Bradshaw, Alex Hebdon, Ann Marie Craig, Isaac Lichlyter, Josh Wheeler, Bobby Woodfin, Michelle Patterson, the Hyles-Anderson College Clinic (thanks for the coffee and popcorn!), Raleigh Aboy, Craig Connor, Dan Petersen, thank you all!

THE PEOPLE WHO MADE MY DREAM COME TRUE

Dave Jorgensen: Thank you for sitting across the table with me, treating me with respect, and taking a chance on a nobody. I hope I get to work with you again in the future.

Linda Stubblefield: You, perhaps more than anyone else, have encouraged me throughout this entire process. Thank you for expertise, hard work, and friendship. You're a remarkable lady.

Pollard Mercer: You got the ball rolling on this project. Thank you for believing in me and for believing that my story should be told.

Doug Wruck, Rena Fish, Dr. David Stubblefield, and the Prepare Now Resource Staff, thank you for the myriad of ways you assisted in this project. I appreciate you all.

THE DIFFERENCE MAKERS

John Cole: You've been a great mentor and leader. You're a man of God, student of the Word, and a friend to me personally. I respect you tremendously and look forward to working with you for a very long time.

Dr. Jack Schaap: You are a man of God in every sense of the term. Thank you for writing the foreword to this book but many more thanks for your passionate preaching, old-fashioned convictions, and compassionate love for people.

Dr. Scott Gray: I was called to preach under your ministry. In many ways you embody what I want to be one day. I admire you and your family immensely.

Dr. Mark Bachman: I've never known a more ardent student of the Word. You challenge me more than you'll ever know. Only eternity will tell the investment you've made in this young man's life and ministry.

Kurt Skelly: I love how you intellectually articulate the Scriptures in such a masterful manner. It is such an honor to have your name associated with this project.

Dr. Bob Gray, II: In truth, you probably should have been the author of this book. God used you to open my eyes so much to His plan for my life. God Bless you—thank you.

Dr. John W. Vaprezsan, Jr: You and your family have been wonderful friends to me. You exemplify true Christianity. Thanks for putting up with and loving "the crippled kid."

Coach Anna Lee: When other people applauded me—you pushed me. Thank you for that. You're perhaps the strongest person I know, and I will always remember the influence you've had on me.

The Staff and Faculty of Hyles-Anderson College: Thank you all for your dedication and sacrifice in your efforts to influence the next generation of Christian leaders.

THE MEDICAL TEAM

Throughout my lifetime, I have known a multitude of doctors, specialists, and nurses. Several of these people have gone above and beyond in their care and concern for me and my family. They will never know how much God used them to be a blessing and encouragement during some of the darkest moments of my life.

A special thanks to...

Dr. Catherine Wood, Missy Carmichael, Dr. Lou Heck, Dr. Tim Beukelman, Dr. Russell Read, Dr. Martin Cogen, Dr. Doug Witherspoon, Brenda Johnson, and Cathy Welch

ABOUT THE AUTHOR

D avid McCroskey's life has been brief and marked by the physical adversity that God has given to him; however, one of David's stated goals has been to live every day to the fullest without allowing anything to ever hold him back. Born in March of 1990 to a Christian family in central Alabama, David is the oldest son of Rodney and Lori McCroskey. The McCroskey family is completed today by David's older sister, Angela (22), as well as younger siblings, Kimberly (16) and Joshua (15).

When he became school age, David was told that he would have to attend special education and classes for the handicapped because of his physical limitations. Believing that such provisions would be unnecessary for their son, Rodney and Lori made the decision to homeschool David and continued to do so all the way through high school graduation. During high school, David was a member of the Eta Sigma Alpha National Honor Society and traveled extensively competing with the National Christian Forensics and Communicators Association. In his three years of competitive debate, David won three national speaking titles and hundreds of state and regional awards. David graduated with a 4.0 GPA and scored in the top five percent in the nation on every achievement and college entrance test taken in high school.

David's interests growing up were always diverse and intensely focused on success. He played basketball for four years as well as placing twice in competitions on a state level as a classical guitarist. With an interest in politics and civil liberties, David was involved as a spokesman for the Arthritis Foundation as well as a speaker for the Tea Party Political Movement.

Currently a senior at Hyles-Anderson College, David has successfully completed his first three years of work on his degree in Youth Ministry in less than two years. At college David has enjoyed working at Lakeshore Baptist Church under the leadership of John Cole as well as having the privilege to preach for men such as Dr. John W. Vaprezsan, Jr. in North Little Rock, Arkansas. After college David plans on pursuing a masters and doctrinal degree while continuing to write and preach.

CONTENTS

FOREWORD

David McCroskey has given his generation a wonderful gift in *The Best Day of Your Life*. Here is a young man who writes with a mature pen—a maturity that comes from his own cup of suffering.

Each generation must have its "life-lesson" teachers. David McCroskey is such a teacher. Through personal anecdotes, Scriptural stories, and mature insight, David leads the reader into a Christ-honoring journey. How I wish a David McCroskey could have been one of Job's three friends.

My prayer is that God will use David's words to touch your heart as they have mine and to encourage and inspire the suffering ones of this generation. Thanks, David

– Dr. Jack Schaap
Pastor, First Baptist Church
Hammond, Indiana

D avid McCroskey is a student in Bible college where I am privileged to teach, but when it comes to facing life's challenges and emerging victoriously, a role reversal takes place: David becomes the teacher, and I am happy to be one of his students. It was with great personal merit that I "sat in David's classroom" by reviewing this manuscript. Refreshingly absent of the stale insipidity typically

expected from the mind of a mere lecturer parroting theories examined in a library from some dusty volume he'd uncovered, the words of this book struck me with the force of compelling power emanating from the heart of an overcomer imparting grace, comfort, and wisdom he'd experienced in the laboratory of a real life he had lived. Any reader willing to "sit at David's feet" will be similarly amazed at the depth and profound impact of every lesson.

– Mark Bachman, *Veteran Missionary*
Faculty, Hyles-Anderson College

I f I were to describe to you the David Mc-Croskey whom I know, you might not be able to recognize him from my description. Some may use words such as "handicapped," "different," or "in need of help." I would have to say "strong," "helpful," "independent," "positive," "happy," "loving," and "dependable."

I'm very happy for everyone who purchases

this book. You are about to enter the life of a very gifted man of God. May you enjoy these pages of great truths.

– Dr. Scott Gray, *Faculty*
Hyles-Anderson College

Insightful. Practical. Helpful. Capturing them skillfully within the context of his own experiences, David McCroskey unveils time-honored Bible truths to help believers of all ages become the conquering Christians God intended for them to be. You will be blessed by this book!

– Pastor Kurt Skelly
Harvest Baptist Church
Natrona Heights, Pennsylvania

INTRODUCTION

by Lori McCroskey

David's life plays in my mind and in my heart as a series of snapshots. On March 26, 1990, our family welcomed a baby boy into the world. The very first picture that I have of our son's life is his daddy sitting in a hospital chair holding a newborn baby and thanking God for the precious gift of a son. David was born full-term and weighed a sturdy 7 pounds, 5 ounces at birth. His Apgar score was a perfect 10, and our little boy seemed healthy in every way. Big sister Angela adored her new playmate immediately, and our little family was very happy.

But the second picture in my mind is of rushing a limp two-week-old to the emergency room where the triage nurse thought that her thermometer must have stopped working. David's temperature registered 106°. The doctor on call quickly pushed us out of the exam room as he performed a spinal tap on our very sick little guy. David had meningitis, and he was immediately admitted to the hospital for treatment. Unknown to us at the time, it was to be the first of many, many hospitalizations for our son. We did not know that emergency rooms, doctors' offices, and therapy centers would become all too familiar to our family in the next years. David did recover from meningitis, but the next snapshot from his life proved to be even scarier for us as young parents.

One early Sunday morning when he was two and a half months old, I picked David up from his crib to nurse him. He smiled up at me from my arms, and I noticed a small bump on his top gum in the front. Over the next few days, the bump doubled and then tripled in size. Alarmed by its rapid growth, we took David to see our pediatrician who told us that she had never seen anything like it before. A few days later as I held David in my lap, I watched in horror as his upper gum split open before my eyes as if an invisible hand was undoing a zipper. There was not a lot of bleeding because the pressure on the gum was so great, but clearly visible inside the opening was a bumpy, very black substance. Within hours, this black mass was protruding from David's gum so much that he could not close his lips. Our pediatrician sent us to an oral surgeon who had never before performed surgery on such a small baby. He removed a section of the black lump for biopsy, telling two very young, very scared parents that he was 90 percent sure that this substance growing so quickly in our son's mouth was a cancerous tumor.

We have a picture from July 4, 1990, of our three-month-old lying on his daddy's chest grinning from ear to ear with a huge, lumpy, black mass sticking out of his mouth. In David's baby book, I have labeled this picture, "Others may see the tumor, but we see the big smile!" For, indeed, it was a tumor although the pathology thankfully came back benign.

Our pediatrician next sent us to see specialists at the University of Alabama Hospital in Birmingham, 90 miles from our home in Montgomery. The final diagnosis for David's tumor was a melanotic neuroectodermal tumor of infancy—a tumor so rare that no one has ever been able to provide us with any information about it or what could have possibly been its cause. This very rapid-growing tumor grew inside the bones of David's face, damaging and literally exploding the bone around it as it grew. David had surgeries to remove this tumor at three months, four months, and six months. We were told before each surgery that this tumor had to be cancerous, although that was never the case. But the tumor left behind much damage.

David is missing a large part of his right cheekbone and the bone designed to support his nose. He also now has a very large cleft palate that is not surgically repairable as congenital cleft palates often can be. Today he wears an obturator that covers the hole in the roof of his mouth and provides him with top teeth, but for 19 years, he lived with a huge cleft in his upper palate and had to learn both to eat and speak with this defect. A bone graft taken from the top of his skull when he was 14 months old failed completely, leaving behind even more damage to the bones in his upper jaw.

There are so many snapshots in my heart from those baby days:

- a tiny baby being sedated time and time again for multiple CT scans and MRIs
- a wonderful nurse breaking all of the rules to sneak me up the back steps into the surgery recovery room at the University of Alabama Hospital so that I could be with my little four-month-old and comfort him
- my heart breaking as I listened to our six-month-old screaming as technicians unsuccessfully tried for literally hours to start an IV on him
- my sweet husband coming home from work several times a day to help with the suctioning of David's airway because it took both of us working together to operate the suction machine and hold down our baby for this task
- our little guy in a special care nursery at Children's Hospital of Alabama, shuffling around the room with IV's in the bottoms of both feet because he had just learned to walk and was determined to show off his new skill
- a 14-month-old with a gash from ear to ear and huge staples across the top of his skull after the failed bone graft.

Most of the time when David was a baby, we felt as if we were fighting to keep him alive. All of the tumor surgeries were treated as emergencies because the tumor's swift growth threatened his right eye and brain as it was destroying his facial bones from the inside out. After each surgery, David was fed intravenously and with feeding tubes into his stomach for a period of time. He developed airway complications several times that first year and was hospitalized and treated for many infections and for chronic croup. David seemed often to be in pain as an infant, although he hardly ever cried. Instead, he slept much more than was normal for a baby, I think as a way for his little body to cope with the pain and infections. My husband and I sat up at night for hours just holding him and listening to him breathe. When he was awake, he smiled—a smile that sometimes broke his parents' hearts and made us turn to our Creator for answers. God gave our family the verse I Kings 8:56 during that first year of David's life—"...*there hath not failed one word of all His good promise....*" We trusted that God is always good and that He loved our baby even more than we did. We kept on trusting the Lord even when our health insurance company bankrupted the summer when David was two years old, leaving us with crushing medical debt that mounted day by day.

David began to walk when he was ten months old, but shortly after the bone graft surgery, he suddenly stopped. We noticed that his knees looked swollen and felt hot to the touch. He was 14 months old when he was given another diagnosis—polyarticular juvenile rheumatoid arthritis. This arthritis has been very cruel to David's body as he has grown up, damaging and destroying the joints of both knees, both ankles, both feet, both wrists, his left elbow, and many fingers and toes. His disease has been both chronic and difficult to treat throughout the years. His rheumatologist at Children's Hospital in Birmingham once told us that David has the worst case of arthritis that he has ever seen in any child.

David's life was filled with persistent pain even as a toddler, especially in the mornings, and we struggled to cope with such a small child dealing with such a devastating disease. I have learned as a mom that it is one thing to see your child ill, but it is another thing entirely to see your child in pain. Before David was two years old, he began both speech therapy twice a week (to deal with his large cleft palate) and physical therapy twice a week (to try to ease the arthritis stiffness and pain). Our family tried every suggestion and every treatment through the years to combat David's arthritis—diets, vitamins, exercises, medications. We made a monthly trip to the Arthritis Clinic at Children's Hospital in Birmingham. Of course, some days with his arthritis were worse than others, but David developed many ways to cope with his pain, including a poignant sense of humor and the ability to laugh at himself when times were tough. He loved bowling and basketball during his elementary years and found ways to compensate for his joints as he played. As he grew, he also found ways to compensate for the speech sounds that he would never be able to make without top teeth. He had wonderful things to say and wanted people to understand him. David was determined that others would see him as a normal kid, not a "handicapped" or "disabled" child, and his daddy determined that we would never tell him "no" whenever he decided to try a new activity. David always managed to find a way to do whatever he wanted to do.

Shortly after David's sixth birthday, a routine eye exam at Children's Hospital in Birmingham revealed that David had developed a complication from his arthritis. He was diagnosed with uveitis in both eyes. Uveitis is an inflammation of the eyes which can lead to blindness. For us, as David's parents, this would prove to be the scariest diagnosis of all. The snapshot in my mind from that day is the ophthalmologist's gripping my shoulder and softly saying, "I am so very sorry, Mrs. McCroskey."

I remember asking the Lord on the drive back to Montgomery that day, "Why? Why does David have to have everything?" The treatment for uveitis is to administer steroid eye drops to the eyes. Because of the severity of David's chronic uveitis, sometimes the doctors prescribed drops for his eyes every hour. We set an alarm clock to go off every hour and tried to continue on with our days. Still, the uveitis and its treatment caused raging glaucoma in both eyes, thick cataracts in both eyes, and retinal detachments in his right eye. David has had seven eye surgeries to place glaucoma shunts in both eyes, remove cataracts from both eyes, and repair detached retinas.

Counting tumor removal and tumor repair surgeries, eye surgeries, and orthopedic surgeries on his knees related to his arthritis, David has had a total of 20 surgeries so far in his life. Our family often joked through the years that David had more surgeries than birthdays. The many procedures, the many tests, and the many, many shots that David has endured through his childhood years are too numerous to count. A six-block section of downtown Birmingham, which contains Children's Hospital of Alabama, the University of Alabama Hospital, and the Callahan Eye Foundation Hospital, became our second home while David was growing up. There were many years we made the three-hour round trip to Birmingham more than sixty times in twelve months.

Here are more of the snapshots in my mind from David's life:

- a three-year-old "army-crawling" through the bedroom in the wee hours of the morning, dragging his legs behind him on his way to the bathroom because his knees and ankles hurt too much to walk

- a four-year-old enduring thick, painful gold shots each week as treatment for his arthritis, joking with the nurse administering the shot and making her laugh
- a five-year-old with furrowed brow concentrating so hard on pleasing his speech therapist
- a seven-year-old who completed most of his second grade schoolwork orally with me because his wrists and hands were so swollen that he could not hold a pencil
- an eight-year-old holding very still as his eye doctor stuck needles into the whites of his eyes to deliver a steroid dose directly into the eyeball
- a nine-year-old who spent a summer on the loveseat in our living room unable to walk on his grossly swollen knees, enduring the indignity and pain of being carried to and from the bathroom
- a ten-year-old who found a way to play his beloved sport of basketball, developing a flat-footed killer "jump" shot that never, ever missed
- an eleven-year-old lying face-down listening to Patch the Pirate tapes for days after retinal detachment surgery in his right eye
- a young teenager conscious of "looking different" who was brave enough to begin public speaking activities, feeling that God had given him a message to deliver and astounding audiences with his way of connecting with others through words
- a seventeen-year-old who courageously faced a facial reconstructive surgery which, of all things, actually made his cleft palate much larger and who lived on whatever Mom could put through the blender for an entire summer
- an older teenager who debated with the third-largest high school forensics league in the country and won three national speaking championships in spite of being the only competitor, out of thousands, who had a cleft palate.

Yes, there are hundreds and hundreds of snapshots in my mind from

David's life. But the clearest picture that will always stay in my heart took place one day when he was 15 years old. That morning as I stood in the kitchen preparing for our family's day, I heard David getting out of bed. It was obviously a "bad" arthritis day. David was hurting. I remember that it took him longer than 15 minutes to walk from his bedroom to the kitchen in our little 1,100-square-foot house that morning. As I listened to him struggle through the living room, moving from one piece of furniture to the next, the thought suddenly occurred to me that David had never once in his entire life known what it was like to wake up in the morning and feel good. My mommy-heart instantly broke, and I began to weep silently over the kitchen sink. David finally arrived at the kitchen door, and he stood behind me holding onto both sides of the door frame for support. He was breathing hard from his efforts, but he said, "Mom! Good morning! It's going to be a great day!"

"Really, David?" I replied. I stood with my back to him, not wanting him to see the tears streaming down my face, and asked, "Is it really going to be a great day?"

"A great day!" he repeated, adding, "I'm pretty sure that this is the best day of my life!" And that statement was David in a nutshell.

Today David walks on severely damaged feet, ankles, and knees. He cannot run or jump as most 20-year-old guys can. Some days it is obvious that he is moving with a great deal of pain, but it is unusual to see him without a smile on his face. Our family has heard David called an "inspiration" more times than his brother and two sisters would like to recall. He has a quick wit and a sometimes slightly sarcastic sense of humor that never fails to make some people laugh and to put others at ease. He has a special empathy for others with health problems that God seems to supply to children who grow up with devastating illness. He has grown up with a desire to help others and to change the world. His daddy once said, "Poor David—all that he ever wanted to be in life was an ordinary kid. But that was impossible because God made him extraordinary."

In the spring of 2008, David's uveitis suddenly turned really ugly, attacking his eyes with a vengeance. As a result, the retina in his right eye, which had already detached, began to repeatedly bubble up and pull apart from the back of his eye. Despite many surgeries, he eventually became blind in that eye in the months to come. That summer, as many of his friends were excitedly making preparations to go off to college in the fall, it became obvious that David would have to delay college. We made two or three trips to Birmingham each week that summer, trying desperately to save his right eye. I remember thinking that, at a time in life when his world should be expanding, suddenly David's world seemed very small. But that August, David spent many hours alone in his room at his desk with his Bible. In a little over a month, he wrote this book. He was 18 years old.

For the last twenty years of David's life, we, as his parents, have prayed three things for him:

1) We have prayed for God to heal our son, for the Lord has never told us to stop praying for this. David has been anointed with oil by several men of God throughout the years, and we will continue to pray with faith each day for God to heal his body.

2) We have prayed that David would not become bitter because of the pain that he has suffered in life.

3) We have prayed that God would somehow use the tremendous health struggles that David has endured for His glory. We pray that this book will be an answer to our third prayer request. Shortly after getting saved, David chose for his life verse II Corinthians 12:9. We pray that, no matter what your "cup" may be in life, the Lord will show you from David's testimony that "...*My grace is sufficient for thee: for my strength is made perfect in weakness....*"

– Lori McCroskey

CHAPTER ONE

YOUR CUP

Foundational Truths Concerning Difficulty

Most people can point to a few critical moments in their life when everything changed. Maybe that change was the birth of a child or a brand-new and exciting opportunity. Perhaps it was a near-death experience or a shocking and unexpected loss. At some time or another, everyone experiences what is commonly termed as a "turning point"—a moment when part of us, or maybe all of us, is forever altered.

I experienced a moment like this one night not long ago when I heard a sermon entitled "Your Cup." I was attending a youth rally at Lighthouse Baptist Church in Theodore, Alabama, pastored by Brother Randy Tewell. That night the preachers were Dr. Scott Gray and his older brother, Dr. Bob Gray II. Brother Scott Gray preached first and then introduced his brother who was going to close out the rally.

When Dr. Bob Gray II stood up and walked behind the pulpit, he explained that he was about to do something that he virtually never did. He said that he was not going to preach the sermon that he had originally intended and planned on preaching that evening. Instead, he was going to preach a sermon that he had never before preached to a group of teenagers. He didn't have the outline to the sermon with him since he had prepared to preach a different sermon, and he simply laid his Bible on the podium and told us all to turn to John chapter 18. Dr. Gray read verses 10 and 11. *"Then Simon Peter having a sword drew it, and smote the high priest's servant, and cut off his right ear. The servant's name was Malchus. Then said Jesus unto Peter, Put up thy sword into the sheath: the cup which my Father hath given me, shall I not drink it?"* Then Dr. Gray began to tell us about his cup.

There wasn't a dry eye in the building as Dr. Gray started to tell of his wonderful son Robert. God has given Robert many serious medical conditions, and his young life has been a constant battle of doctors, surgeries, and dangerous situations. Pouring out his heart and soul that night, Dr. Gray told us of the trials and hardships that he and his wife had endured because of Robert's medical conditions. He explained that his son Robert was his "cup." Just like Christ had a burden and a struggle with which to contend, so did Dr. Gray. Christ's cup was to suffer and die for the sins of all mankind. Dr. Gray's cup was a son who would always demand constant monitoring and endless medical procedures.

Everyone in attendance that evening laughed and cried openly while listening spellbound to a devoted father expound the depth of love that he possessed for his special son—his cup. I've never witnessed a room of people (especially teenagers) be so emotionally and spiritually affected in my life. The altars were packed, and lives were changed. I had a three-hour-long drive home that night, and all that I could think about was that sermon. Actually, that sermon was all I could think about for days. My friends who were with me that night were affected in the same way that I was. What a special night!

God, through Dr. Gray, opened my eyes to truths and thoughts that I had never before seen. That rally was doubtless a turning point in my life—a portion of the will of God was revealed to me that evening. All of it centered around this thought of a "cup." Please allow me to share several truths concerning "cups" while we are just beginning this journey in order to lay the groundwork for all that I want to address and accomplish within the pages of this book.

What Is a Cup?

Have you ever noticed in life that it can be very important to define the terms that you are using? Many bitter contentions and arguments could have been easily avoided if the parties who were upset with each other would have taken the time to get on the same page and define exactly the terms that they were using. Consider a dad who tells his son to clean the family car. The son, wanting to please and obey his father, immediately goes outside and washes and waxes the car. The next day, however, the father expresses his displeasure and disappointment to his son that the car is not clean.

The son is confused. In his mind, he has done everything to satisfy his dad's request, and he is truly bewildered as to why his father is upset with him. The two argue back and forth with each other until the father finally says something that makes the son realize why his dad isn't happy with his work. His dad mentions that the trash inside the car was not picked up, and neither were the seats vacuumed. It dawns on the son that his dad wanted him to care for the interior of the car as well as the exterior. The confusion and contention could have been easily avoided if the dad and the son would have defined the term "clean."

Obviously, the father's definition of the phrase "clean the car" meant to take care of both the interior and exterior of the vehicle. However, the son's definition solely meant the outside of the car. Neither father nor son was really in the wrong. Their misunderstanding was caused simply because of a lack of clarity.

Maybe you've gotten yourself into a few embarrassing situations because of a lack of clear understanding or because your definition was different than someone else's. With this thought in mind, I think it is very important for me to define what exactly I mean when I refer to a person's "cup." May I share first what is NOT a cup.

Sin Is Not a Cup

Realizing that sin is not a cup is very crucial because a misunderstanding at this point could be catastrophic. Do not ever look at a perpetual sin problem in your life and make the mistake of thinking that it is a cup that has been given to you by God. If you are reading this book because you want to learn how to live and cope with a besetting sin, then you have picked up the wrong piece of literature.

A cup is given to an individual by God; therefore, it is a singular trial or event that a person receives involuntarily. We can't help it, so to speak. Dr. Gray could not help that his son was born with complicated medical issues. I couldn't help having a tumor, rheumatoid arthritis, or uveitis. In a sense, a cup is forced upon you. You get it whether or not you like it.

However, God has never and will never force someone to sin. And for you to excuse your sin by saying that God has given it to you for whatever reason is just plain wrong. James 1:13-16 says,

> "Let no man say when he is tempted, I am tempted of God: for God cannot be tempted with evil, neither tempteth he any man: 14But every man is tempted, when he is drawn away of his own lust, and enticed. 15Then when lust hath conceived, it bringeth forth sin: and sin, when it is finished, bringeth forth death. 16Do not err, my beloved brethren."

These verses make it abundantly clear that sin in our lives is not given to us by God—and therefore cannot be classified as a cup because of the context of the Scripture and the following verses.

I actually think this passage comes across as quite stern. The word *tempted* in verse 13 is referring to the temptation to sin. We know this because the verse says, *"Let no man say when he is tempted, I am tempted of God."* What is the Bible saying? This portion of Scripture wraps up with a parting warning in verse 16, *"Do not err, my beloved brethren."* Don't blame your sin problem on God! Never say, "I'm just not able to rid myself of this sin issue because God has placed it into my life for a reason." I don't think so.

We sin because we are fallen humans—not because God has forced it upon us. That truth is quite elementary. Genesis 6:5 describes where sin originates. *"And God saw that the wickedness of man was great in the earth, and that every imagination of the thoughts of his heart was only evil continually."* The wicked heart of man conceives and executes sin—not the perfect will of God. I believe God's attitude toward sin is summed up in I John 1:9. *"If we confess our sins, he is faithful and just to forgive us our sins, and to cleanse us from all unrighteousness."*

If God brought sin into our lives for a reason, then why would He be willing to forgive us of sin and to cleanse us from all unrighteousness every single time we asked Him to do that in our lives? Obviously sin is not something God uses to work in our lives. Our sin is not a cup. Don't misunderstand that point. There is one more point that I must address on what a cup is not.

A Cup Is Not a Result of Sin

The summer when I was nine years old was a dark time in my household. At the very beginning of the summer, I came down with a serious virus that was unlike most viral infections. This one didn't go away. I soon reached the point where all I had the strength to do was lie on the couch. The fever that I was running meant that I could not take much of my arthritis medication, and I soon found myself unable to walk or stand under my own power. For months my poor mom had to carry me to and from the bathroom. I spent parts of that summer in a state of delirium.

The truth is that almost everything I am sharing is by way of my parents because I don't actually remember much of that summer at all. The only time I left the house was to get in a wheelchair and go to a doctor's office where the medical world struggled in vain to find the source of what was quite literally draining the life from my body. One thing I do remember is being tired—incredibly tired. I literally slept away the summer. Finally, the doctors admitted me to Children's Hospital in Birmingham, Alabama. There the cause of the virus was finally discovered, and then I began my road to recovery.

Obviously, we didn't get out much that summer. At first people were really fantastic about coming by and checking on Mom and me, but as the length of the illness kept extending, the trail of well-wishers started to fade. One afternoon, however, my mom received a call from a church lady we knew. She expressed her concern for my health, but sadly, she didn't stop there. She went on to inform Mom that if she and my dad would confess the sin in their life that I would get better. With a few misguided words, this lady had placed the entire responsibility for my sickness on what she perceived as a sin problem in my parents' life.

Allow me to share a few thoughts on that instance. First, it was not her place to judge my parents. Secondly, hers were not comforting words. Thirdly, my parents had already contemplated the possibility that this extended medical problem could be the judgment of God. Trust me, they didn't need someone else to perpetuate that thought.

The truth is that my parents had already begged God to show them if there was something in their life that was causing my continual illness.

However, God never revealed anything to my parents. My sickness that summer was a temporary cup that God brought into the life of my family—not the result of sin in anyone's life.

Many times a trial or hardship comes into a person's life because God has a grander plan in mind and not because God is trying to get that person's attention about a sin problem. The Word of God clears up this common misconception in John 9:1-3:

"And as Jesus passed by, he saw a man which was blind from his birth. ²And his disciples asked him, saying, Master, who did sin, this man, or his parents, that he was born blind? ³Jesus answered, Neither hath this man sinned, nor his parents: but that the works of God should be made manifest in him."

This man's blindness—his cup, if you please—wasn't because of his sin or because of sins that his parents had committed. He was blind so *"... that the works of God should be made manifest in him."*

How do you know if the trial or hardship that you are experiencing is the judgment of the Almighty or a cup intended for your good and the glory of God? The Just One will reveal that answer to you. A just God could not punish you without first letting you know why He was doing so. When God was about to judge David for his sin with Bathsheba, He first sent the prophet Nathan to make it clear to David why he was being punished. II Samuel 12:14 says, *"Howbeit, because by this deed thou hast given great occasion to the enemies of the LORD to blaspheme, the child also that is born unto thee shall surely die."* The death of David and Bathsheba's son was judgment for sin. The child's death was not a cup; a cup is not the result of sin.

So back to the original question: what is a cup? A *cup* is "any trial, hardship, or limitation that God brings into one's life."

- It's the loss of a child.
- It's a devastating disease.
- It's a friend who shuns you in your time of need.
- It's the loss of a job.
- It's being abused or misused.
- It can be tangible.

- It can be intangible.
- It can be physical.
- It can be emotional.
- It can be temporary.
- It can be permanent.
- It always hurts.
- It's never easy.
- It's the event that brings you to your knees.
- It's the circumstance that tests your strength.
- It's the news that leaves you cold and out of breath.

I don't know what the cup is in your life. You do. You know your cup. Let me share a few universal truths about cups.

Everyone Has a Cup

I believe one of our biggest temptations when we look at the problems in our life is to think that we are alone. We have a natural inclination to feel isolated and separated from everyone else. This thought process causes us to forget that we have an everlasting God Who will never leave us nor forsake us. The truth is, though, that most of the time we aren't quite as alone as we might be tempted to think. Hardship is universal. No one has ever been spared the pain of a trial. Every person who has ever walked the earth has known pain and sorrow. No exceptions. Nobody gets left out. In the midst of a storm, it is fairly common to hear someone express the sentiment that "nobody understands" what he is going through. Sometimes that is true.

As I write this chapter, I just heard about a four-year-old boy who has been diagnosed with terminal cancer. I cannot relate to that; I don't even have kids. The pain that those parents are experiencing is foreign to me. Despite my best efforts to understand and comprehend, I just can't. In general, however, the pain, the agony, the confusion, and the fear that those poor parents are currently experiencing is all too common for everyone.

Everyone has a cup. We can all point to that thing, and probably for most those things, that we would call the defining troubles or heartaches of our life. Look at the Bible. Practically everyone whose life the Word of God spends any amount of time chronicling had a cup. Moses had a speech impediment that he believed would hinder him from leading the children of Israel out of Egypt. Abraham had a nephew who broke his heart. Paul had a thorn in his flesh (I personally think it was rheumatoid arthritis.) Job had his wealth and his family taken from him in an instant. Adam and Eve had one of their sons kill the other one. David had a son who tried to take his kingdom. Noah was mocked and derided tirelessly for several decades. Joseph was sold into slavery by his own family, then falsely accused and wrongly imprisoned. The list goes on and on.

Allow me to turn from Biblical examples and think about just a few of the people whom I know personally. My grandmother was killed by a drunk driver when my dad was just 13 years old. My mother is dealing with both of her parents having cancer at the same time. My mind wanders to a teenage boy who was molested when he was 12 years old. I now turn to a good Christian father who has had every one of his children break his heart and turn from the values that he tried so hard to instill in them. I could go on for pages. I can assure you that in each case, the person with the cup didn't choose the circumstance or situation. It just happened—not by accident, mind you. It happened because God allowed it. It's their cup.

We all have one. Take a moment and think about yours. You know what it is, don't you? Of course. I know what mine is, too. You aren't alone. We're all in this together.

I have established that we all have one, but that doesn't mean all cups are equal. In fact, quite the opposite is true.

All Cups Are Unique

I live in Alabama where we fondly tell people that we have four seasons: very hot, unbearably hot, still hot, and Christmas. Yep, it's hot, my friends. It's always hot. The worst season by far is the "still-hot" season. This one, which spans September and November, is just hard to handle physiologically and mentally. When you walk out of the house on an October afternoon, you just expect it to be cool and comfortable.

When that vicious blast of heat and humidity hits you and sucks the air out of your lungs, it feels even worse than it should because you were expecting better! I've lived in the heart of Dixie my entire life, and I can recall it snowing three times. In general, when it snows in the South, things get quite comical. My mom (who grew up in Minnesota) laughs as our entire city shuts down over a few flurries. As a younger kid, however, I always looked forward to going outside and playing in the snow. We would roll around in the snow, play for hours, and of course, have endless snowball fights. Just for the record, I always won!

All that to say, I have limited experience and knowledge when it comes to snowflakes. Of course, I have heard that no two snowflakes are alike. If that's true, snowflakes and heartaches have something in common. No two cups are just exactly alike either. They come in all different shapes and sizes. If for no other reason, every burden is unique because every person is unique. The way that a particular trial hits one person will be different from the way it affects someone else just simply because the two people are unique individuals who will react to the exact same circumstance in different ways.

This truth is important to understand because it will affect how we handle the limitations or problems that God brings into our life. The realization that the cup God has given us is different from anyone else's is so crucial to understanding that our cup provides certain unique opportunities for us to grow and serve God. I now want to explore two very different and broad categories of cups.

Some Cups Are Temporary

In Daniel chapter three some young men were faced with a temporary cup. Shadrach, Meshach, and Abednego were faced with a fiery (literally) trial. King Nebuchadnezzar had erected a golden image of himself and commanded that all of the rulers and officers of his kingdom bow down and worship his idol. Three young Jewish rulers, Shadrach, Meshach, and Abednego, refused to obey the commandment of the king. They knew that to bow in worship to a graven image was detestable in the sight of God.

What was the designated penalty for this insubordination? Death by way of a burning furnace. Let me point out that these three Jewish rulers didn't do anything wrong. In fact, Shadrach, Meshach, and Abednego took a tremendous stand against idolatry. So once again, being thrown in the fiery furnace was certainly not the judgment of God. It was a hard trial—a cup—that was involuntary forced upon them. But let me point out that theirs was a temporary cup. Daniel 3:23-26 reveals the conclusion of the hardship.

> "And these three men, Shadrach, Meshach, and Abednego, fell down bound into the midst of the burning fiery furnace. ²⁴Then Nebuchadnezzar the king was astonied, and rose up in haste, and spake, and said unto his counsellers, Did not we cast three men bound into the midst of the fire? They answered and said unto the king, True, O king. ²⁵He answered and said, Lo, I see four men loose, walking in the midst of the fire, and they have no hurt; and the form of the fourth is like the Son of God. ²⁶Then Nebuchadnezzar came near to the mouth of the burning fiery furnace, and spake, and said, Shadrach, Meschach, and Abednego, ye servants of the most high God, come forth, and come hither. Then Shadrach, Meschach, and Abednego, came forth of the midst of the fire."

In just a matter of moments, deliverance had arrived. Theirs was a temporary cup.

Not every trial lasts a lifetime. Some are just for a few hours, maybe weeks, potentially years, but eventually they end. When I think about a temporary burden in my family, I am reminded of the medical debt that was referenced in the introduction of this book. That burden was hard. My entire family was affected, but especially my two wonderful parents who were very limited and burdened by the crush of debt that they found themselves under. But the bottom line is that as of today only a few thousand dollars remains to be paid. Thanks to God's provision and my father's incredible work ethic, my family will finally climb out of the abyss of medical debt. Theirs will be a temporary cup.

Some Cups Are Permanent

Contrary to a trial or limitation that ends within a certain amount of time, there are moments when God sees fit to give a person a burden that never goes away. It can be a small inconvenience, or it can be a major part of one's life until the day that person dies. But no matter what it is, it's permanent.

I'm thinking about a friend of mine right now who has been given a permanent limitation. Chris is 18 years old, and he is perhaps the most talented person I know. Chris is arguably the best soccer player in our state. He is a prolific public speaker and a national champion debater. His intelligence levels are off the charts, and he could persuade Eskimos to buy ice. Just to top it off, he sings like Frank Sinatra and is the most likable and friendly person whom you could ever hope to meet. But many people do not know that Chris has a limitation. He is completely blind in one eye. Due to an accident earlier in his life, he will never again be able to see out of one of his eyes.

Now let me say that Chris handles this God-given limitation with a tremendous amount of acceptance and grace. He wears a shell that looks like a real eye over what is, to put it bluntly, the "remains" of his original eye. To the casual onlooker, it is nearly impossible to tell that he cannot see out of that eye. And Chris never makes a big deal out of it. I only found out about his condition when another one of his friends casually mentioned it to me one day. Chris doesn't allow his blindness to define him or limit him, but the fact of the matter is that his lack of eyesight will forever be a limitation in his life.

Sometimes, for His reasons and purposes, God sees fit to give people troubles or pain that will never go away. In my life, the rheumatoid arthritis that God gave me many years ago will be a permanent cup. Short of God's taking it from me in a miraculous fashion, it's not going away. I'll never reach the point where I am completely uninhibited by its effects on my body.

Paul, the great apostle and missionary, also had a permanent cup that affected his body. He speaks most eloquently about his physical limitation in II Corinthians chapter twelve.

"And lest I should be exalted above measure through the abundance of the revelations, there was given to me a thorn in the flesh, the messenger of Satan to buffet me, lest I should be exalted above measure. ⁸For this thing I besought the Lord thrice, that it might depart from me. ⁹And he said unto me, My grace is sufficient for thee: for my strength is made perfect in weakness. Most gladly therefore will I rather glory in my infirmities, that the power of Christ may rest upon me." (II Corinthians 12:7-9)

For three seasons of time, Paul begged God to take away his "thorn in the flesh," but each and every time God came back with the answer "no." Every indication is given that this limitation was never removed from Paul's life, and it was a cup he was forced to deal with on a daily basis.

From a purely physiological viewpoint, a permanent weakness is the hardest kind to handle. Many people are, by nature, "fixers." In essence, they want to make things right. They want to fix or mend. But sometimes the weakness just cannot be fixed. Chris can't change his blindness. I can't change my arthritis. Paul couldn't change his limitation. In each instance, the challenge was meant by God to be a lasting one.

You Have to Drink Your Cup

Destiny. That word can be pretty daunting, can't it? Destiny is the thought that there is some mystical, magical purpose that we are all supposed to fulfill during our lifetime. It can be especially frightening to a teenager since so much of his destiny is still a clouded mystery. If you are 40 or 50 years old, you probably have a pretty good idea of what your destiny has turned out to be. You know where you went to college. You know who you were supposed to marry. You know whether or not you were supposed to have children. You probably have your career field determined. Perhaps you've been stable in the same church for years, and you know that's where God wants you and your family to attend. You've got somewhat of a grip on this destiny matter.

I'm jealous because I don't know. At the time of this writing, where I'm going to college, if or whom I'll marry, and where I'll end up living are all yet to be determined in my life. I'd love to know all of that. I'd really like to be able to sit down and read a piece of paper that outlines exactly what I can expect for the rest of my life. I've always been the type of person who likes to know what's coming. I don't mind surprises, but I don't want to know that a surprise is coming either because then I get anxious. Just let it happen, and then I'll be excited. I like to plan. I like to know what's coming next. That's just not how God works though. God reveals His will for our life one little step at a time.

Much of what happens in life is up to us. To a certain extent, we have a say in how our life goes. For example, I could choose to completely wreck and ruin my life and my destiny tomorrow. That would be a pretty foolish decision, but I could probably do it if I tried hard enough. Some things about our life, however, are completely out of our realm of control or influence. The challenges and difficulties that we face in life are most often out of our hands. A child born with a severe medical condition is not born that way because of a choice or a decision he made. My friend Chris can't help being blind in one of his eyes. My grandmother's being killed by a drunken driver when my dad was just 13 years old was not something that anyone would have chosen. We don't get the luxury of choosing the trials that we experience. It's all up to God and His perfect design and will for each of our individual lives.

The bottom line: we have to drink our cup. We can't pass. We can't politely say, "No, thank You." We can't run. We can't hide. We can't pretend it isn't happening. We can't trade with someone else. We have to drink our cup. This is a major part of accepting (and then embracing and utilizing) the challenges God has given to us.

Too many people ruin their lives because they refuse to drink their cup. Sadly, many people take their lives because they refuse to drink their cup. Many people turn to alcohol, illicit drugs, or prescription medicine trying to cope with pain that only God can help them handle. But what some don't seem to realize is that after all the drinking, the drugs, and the medication, the heartache still remains. Nothing that we can do will make the cup disappear. There it sits in front of us. We have to drink our cup.

Don't get too depressed on me yet, though. The fact that we have to drink our cup is just that—a fact. Yes, it is a fact that must be acknowledged and realized, but it obviously doesn't stop there. It's not as elementary as just attempting to survive your cup. God wants us to thrive in our trials. That's one of the reasons why He gives us cups to drink from in the first place. So don't close the book yet. God has some very exciting and comforting truths! In fact, I am about to share one!

All Cups Are Given by God

I realize that I am probably overflowing with bias on the subject, but I honestly believe that God has blessed me with one of the best sets of parents a child has ever had. My parents have always loved and cared for me in the best way possible. They have never been wealthy people, but both of them have always tried to do special things to let their children know how much they care. Looking back on all of the gifts and presents that they have given to me over the years, I am struck by the thought that they have always given me good things. Nothing that has ever been transferred from their ownership to mine has been to or for my detriment. While growing up, whenever I would look under the Christmas tree at all of the wrapped presents, I never wondered if one of the presents would make me miserable or tempt me to be a bad person. Of course not! I always knew that if the present was coming from my parents, then it was going to be for my good.

Herein is the exciting and comforting part: every cup is given to us by God! John 18:11b says, *"Put up thy sword into the sheath: the cup which my Father hath given me, shall I not drink it?"* This verse plainly says the cup came from God. The cup was ordained, prepared, and given by God Himself. Where do the cups in our life come from? You guessed it! The thought that my cup was prepared for me at the hand of God really is a tremendous comfort to me personally. God never looks down at our lives and says, "Uh, oh." He is never surprised or taken offguard by our circumstances. Rather, He in His infinite knowledge has specifically placed those challenges in our lives according to His plan. Christ remarks in Matthew 10:30, *"But the very hairs of your head are all numbered."* If God takes the time to keep track of how many hairs are on each person's head, then He obviously pays great attention to the heartaches and difficulties as well!

This truth excites me beyond comprehension! Satan didn't give me my arthritis; God allowed it. The Devil wasn't in control of my tumor. God was. Whatever the burden that you bear happens to be, God gave it to you. This is so important because this truth gives us the assurance that our cup is meant for our good! God will always give us challenges that are meant to strengthen and help us just like He gave my parents one for their good. Jeremiah 29:11 says, *"For I know the thoughts that I think toward you, saith the LORD, thoughts of peace, and not of evil, to give you an expected end."* God doesn't sit up in Heaven and devise ways to make our life miserable. He has *"thoughts of peace"* in mind when He contemplates the events of our lives. The problem that we as human beings run into is that we don't have the perspective or insight that an omniscient God possesses. That is why we so often view the hardships in our life as negatives when the truth is that they are meant for our good. Since we do not understand why God brings the heartache into our life, we don't accept it either. Truly, the only thing that we really need to understand is that our Father, Who created us and loved us enough to send His Son to die in our stead, would not give us a burden with the intention of harming us.

This truth is also so crucial because it helps us further understand that God is in control. He's the One Who gave us the trial; therefore, He is also the One Who can help us accept, embrace, and use the trial for our benefit and His glory. As Christ was talking to Peter about why He wasn't fighting His cup, the only reason that Jesus felt was worthy of enumerating at the time was that His Father had given Him the cup. In Christ's mind, that knowledge was more than enough reason to accept it and embrace it. Christ didn't say, "Peter, I have to die because it is going to provide salvation for all of mankind." No, Christ said, *"The cup which my Father hath given me, shall I not drink it?"* It is so vital that we recognize at the beginning from where exactly it is that we received our cup in the first place.

You Can Handle Your Cup

This is one truth that you just have to pound into your conscious mind. You can handle your cup. When I say that you can handle your cup, I don't mean that you alone are capable of dealing with the challenges by yourself. I mean that through the grace and strength of Jesus Christ, you can absolutely conquer the challenges that God has seen fit to give to you. You can drink from your cup.

My mom has always had a saying that has stayed with me throughout my life: "You can do what you have to do." That statement is so true. It's true for a couple of different reasons.

First of all, you can do what you have to do because God would not give us a challenge that He knows will be too much for us. Why? Because it's not possible. God cannot give us something that we aren't capable of handling because He can handle anything. If we remember always to turn to Him in our time of crisis and need, then we can always handle our burden. I'm not trying to promote a "self-help, you-can-do-it" philosophy. I'm trying to present quite the opposite actually. You can't do it; I can't do it. But through God and with His help, we can. The Bible makes it clear that man alone cannot handle the situations of life, but with God there is nothing too hard. Matthew 19:26 says, *"But Jesus beheld them, and said unto them, With men this is impossible; but with God all things are possible."* If we believe on Christ and His abilities, then we ourselves are empowered though Him. Mark 9:23 explains, *"Jesus said unto him, If thou canst believe, all things are possible to him that believeth."*

Through God we can handle our cup. Think back to Paul and the challenge that God gave to him. When he sought for God to take away his "thorn," God responded by saying, *"...My grace is sufficient for thee...."* What was God saying? He was saying, "Paul, you can handle your cup." *"I can do all things through Christ which strengtheneth me."* (Philippians 4:13)

Christ Had to Accept His Cup

When the soldiers came to take Him away, He didn't put up a fight. He surrendered to the will of His Father. He was beaten, scourged, mocked, and cursed. His body was bloody and drenched in the sweat of a suffering man. Everyone who was close to Him on earth turned his back and fled in fear. He was put through a mockery of a trial and was chosen to be put to death instead of a known criminal. He was given vinegar to drink and a crown of thorns to wear. He was hung on the Cross all alone—even His Father had to turn away. He was killed for sins that He had never committed. That was Christ's cup.

What came of that cup? What was the reason? Why did Christ have to drink that cup? Jesus accepted His cup so that on January 8, 1997, I could ask God to forgive my sins, save me, and give me an eternal dwelling place in Heaven. I thank God every single day that He gave Christ a cup. I thank God every day that Christ accepted His cup. Without that cup, I would have no way to atone for my sins. You wouldn't either. I'm so happy that Christ accepted His cup as the will of God for His life. I'm so grateful that Christ embraced His cup as a gift from His Father. I am ever thankful that Christ used His cup as a means to provide for the salvation of the world.

There is a reason for your challenges, too. No, you will not save anyone from Hell by going through your trial, but you just might encourage, inspire, or uplift someone who is experiencing the same pain as you are. You might just make an eternal difference in someone's life. But before you can do any of that, you have to take the first step that Christ did. You have to accept your cup. You have to drink it. You have to look at it from a Godly perspective and realize that it is God's will for your life. You have to understand that your cup is a gift from your Heavenly Father because He wants to show you something or take you somewhere that you cannot go without first going through the fiery trial.

I beg you to take the first step and accept whatever it is that God in His wisdom has placed in your life that could be considered a cup. Accept that your cup, whether temporary or permanent, is a unique opportunity to be used of God. Accept that your cup is the will of God for your life. Accept that you have to drink your cup. Accept and realize that through Christ and His grace…you can handle your cup.

Christ accepted His cup. The least we can do is the same.

I am forever indebted to Dr. Bob Gray II for opening my eyes to such magnificent truths about my "cup."

*"The cup of suffering
is not the same size
for everyone."*

CHAPTER TWO

WHY?

Answering the Unavoidable Questions

I have always been a fan of major sports. I have often told people that I'll watch or play anything that involves a ball. Keep in mind though that I just excluded gymnastics, ice skating, and hockey. Sorry, but I just don't get that excited about those three "sports." I will, to be honest with you though, admit that I am the kind of person who tries to catch Sportscenter every morning. My favorite sport by far has always been basketball.

There was a time in my life when I lived and breathed what I considered to be "the" game. I used to shoot over 500 jump shots a day. My mom would have to force me to come inside for dinner from practicing every evening. Looking back, I think the Christmas gifts about which I became the most excited were an official leather basketball and my first ever basketball goal from my parents. I grew up during the Michael Jordan era in the National Basketball Association (NBA). Consequently, I soon joined the multitude and became a Chicago Bulls fan. To this day, if I thought about it, I could probably recite the entire Bulls roster during the 1996 season when they set a still-standing league record by going 72-10 in the regular season.

Obviously, stemming from my love of basketball was my desire to play on an organized team. Between the ages of eight and twelve, I was blessed enough to fulfill that desire. Because of my physical limitations, I was never the best player, but neither was I ever the worst. The Lord blessed me with good coaches who knew how to minimize my weaknesses and maximize my strengths. I couldn't run fast enough to keep up with the other players, but I learned how to anticipate what was going to happen in enough time for me to compensate for my lack of agility. When the ball was shot, instead of crashing the boards for the rebound, I would start backpedaling toward the other side of the court to make sure I was in position for the ensuing possession. It eventually reached the point where I honestly believe that my arthritis didn't inhibit the team much at all. The teams for which I played went a combined 25-6-1 in the four years that I competed.

The last year that I played basketball, however, I had to face the facts about my situation. My teammates were getting stronger and faster. I knew I would not be able to keep up in just a matter of time. It wouldn't matter what little tricks I tried to implement. Everything inside of me wanted to keep playing basketball all through high school, but I knew that desire wouldn't be fair to the team for which I played. No matter how well I could handle the ball or hit an open jumper, I was always going to hold back the team because of my lack of athleticism. I realized for the sake of my fellow players and the good of the team that I had to give up organized, competitive basketball.

That was a hard decision to make because I love basketball, and I love to compete. Having to give up an activity that involved both of these aspects was difficult. Most teenage guys do not have to make the decision that I did. Most young people have the opportunity to participate in some form of organized athletics and never have to stop because of a physical limitation. Maybe they have to stop because of a job, or school, or church...but not because of rheumatoid arthritis, right? The temptation for me was to look around at all of the kids who were able to play whatever sport they wanted and think that somehow I was being left out. I was being cheated. I was even tempted to think that my situation wasn't fair. I wanted to look toward Heaven and with a frustrated heart ask "Why?"

The immediate response to a perceived burden in our life is to wonder and ask "Why?" The questions are endless.

- Why me?
- Why do people suffer?
- Why does God allow this?
- Why isn't life easier?
- Why does it hurt so much?

These questions and others like them are unavoidable and many times seemingly unanswerable.

I believe it's important for a person to take an honest and perhaps painful look at this question of "Why?" before one can really accept the trials of his life. The person with a cup needs to shine a bright light on this question and answer a few "why" questions of his own while he is at it.

- Why do people ask "Why?"
- When will a person know the reason behind his pain?
- What good can come from one's suffering?
- And finally, why does God afflict His children?

I don't pretend to think that I can answer all of the questions which plague a person's mind when he is faced with the storm of his life. What afflicts another is a mystery to me. Therefore, it is impossible for me to determine the grand reason and purpose behind another's suffering. But even if I did know what it is that another person would consider the hardships and heartaches of his life, it wouldn't change the fact that I cannot read the mind of God. He works in miraculous and many times mysterious ways, my friend. Much of what He does is never for us to know or understand, but the Word of God does provide many clues and much penetrating insight behind God's reasoning as to why He allows a burden or limitation to enter a person's life. Please read this chapter with an open mind and a prayerful heart. Perhaps God will reveal to you a little bit of the mind of Christ.

People Ask "Why?" Because They Don't Trust God

"Now the LORD had said unto Abram, Get thee out of thy country, and from thy kindred, and from thy father's house, unto a land that I will shew thee: ²And I will make of thee a great nation, and I will bless thee, and make thy name great; and thou shalt be a blessing: ³And I will bless them that bless thee, and curse him that curseth thee: and in thee shall all families of the earth be blessed. ⁴So Abram departed, as the LORD had spoken unto him; and Lot went with him: and Abram was seventy and five years old when he departed out of Haran. ⁵And Abram took

Sarai his wife, and Lot his brother's son, and all their substance that they had gathered, and the souls that they had gotten in Haran; and they went forth to go into the land of Canaan; and into the land of Canaan they came." (Genesis 12:1-5)

Genesis chapter twelve contains a truly remarkable story of God's visiting Abram and telling him in no uncertain terms to leave his country immediately. Here's the hard part: God never told Abram where he was going. Knowing the destination is an important part of a trip, isn't it? The eventual destination is not normally something that is left a mystery at the beginning of a journey. I know of a family who once took a vacation with no destination in mind. The family piled into their van and laid down one simple rule: anyone for any reason could stop the van. The lady telling me about the vacation noted that they never made it more than 50 miles away from their house the entire first day! For obvious reasons, that's not normally the way that traveling plans are made! Typically in fact, the end point of the trip is one of the first things decided upon. God, though, just doesn't operate the way that human beings do.

Two key phrases from Genesis 12:1-5 reveal the amazing part of the story. *"...Get thee out of thy country...So Abram departed...."* God said, "Get thee out," and Abram "departed." For Abram it was that simple—no long discussion, no argument, and no question "Why?"

Think for a moment what all God was ordering Abram to do. Abram was to completely uproot his family, his life, and his belongings in order to move to a location that God would tell him about later. If there was ever a time to ask "Why?" this was it! So how was Abram able to endure hardship and inconvenience with such apparent contentment? The answer is simple: he trusted God...completely. *"And he [Abram] believed in the LORD; and he counted it to him for righteousness."* (Genesis 15:6) Abram didn't have to question God because he *"...believed in the LORD."* He had the assurance that God would never lead him somewhere or place him in a situation without a great purpose and a great plan. The New Testament further explains exactly why Abram didn't play "20 questions" with God. *"By faith Abraham, when he was called to go out into a place which he should after receive for an inheritance, obeyed; and he went out, not knowing whither he went.*" (Hebrews 11:8)

Abraham didn't ask "Why?" because he had total confidence that God knew what He was doing and how He was orchestrating Abraham's life. It's kind of harsh to think about, but in all honesty, the reason why we question God is that we don't trust Him. I am not attempting to throw stones at you personally. Please don't think that I am. Trust me, I empathize with your searching. I have lain awake at night crying… wondering…asking. I know. I understand that natural reaction of crying out in illogical anguish. Sometimes pain and disappointment can overpower our faith in Christ. However, it is of the utmost importance that we force ourselves to take a deep breath, step back, and reflect upon the omniscience of God when we are tempted to question His goodness. We have to remember that it is not our job to understand and agree with the circumstances that He decides are best for us. Romans 9:20 gives a very logical reminder to the person who disagrees with God's plan for his life. *"Nay but, O man, who art thou that repliest against God? Shall the thing formed say to him that formed it, Why hast thou made me thus?"*

This verse gives us a very stern, yet helpful admonishment. No person has the right to question God's design for his life. He created us! The Creator gets to decide what He does with His creation. That's the way it works—especially if you are a child of the King. *"What? know ye not that your body is the temple of the Holy Ghost which is in you, which ye have of God, and ye are not your own? For ye are bought with a price: therefore glorify God in your body, and in your spirit, which are God's."* (I Corinthians 6:19, 20) We aren't our own; we are bought with a price—a very expensive price at that. If we would have created and then saved ourselves, we might deserve a little bit of say-so in how our life unfolds. But since there isn't an honest person alive who can claim either of those accomplishments, it really is our responsibility to trust the One Who cared enough about us to create us and then loved us enough to die in our place. *"The LORD is righteous in all his ways, and holy in all his works."* (Psalm 145:17)

People Ask "Why?" to Express Pain, Not Because They Want to Understand

I have learned this truth as I have observed not only my life but also the lives of those around me. Many times when a person (whether honestly or bitterly) cries out in a frustrated and confused question-laced tirade, he doesn't really want to know why. He doesn't necessarily want to understand or comprehend. Rather, he is simply seeking an avenue to let out the pain and hurt that he is experiencing. Wanting to express his agony in some tangible format is oftentimes the true source of our questioning—not because we hate God or His will for our life.

When I think about this truth, I am reminded of the Psalmist David. Here was someone who was called a man after God's own heart—not a perfect man but a very godly man. He was a giant of the faith and one of the most prominently documented members of the Old Testament. However, if you read some of the Psalms that David wrote without knowing the entirety of his life, it would be very easy to believe that he was nothing more than a bitter and disgruntled man. Psalm 77:3-9 says,

"I remembered God, and was troubled: I complained, and my spirit was overwhelmed. Selah. ⁴Thou holdest mine eyes waking: I am so troubled that I cannot speak. ⁵I have considered the days of old, the years of ancient times. ⁶I call to remembrance my song in the night: I commune with mine own heart: and my spirit made diligent search. ⁷Will the LORD cast off for ever? and will he be favourable no more? ⁸Is his mercy clean gone for ever? doth his promise fail for evermore? ⁹Hath God forgotten to be gracious? hath he in anger shut up his tender mercies? Selah."

The same sweet Psalmist who penned some of the most beautiful words ever recorded in human history about God and His mercy seems to have completely lost trust in Him and His nature. I believe David sounds bitter in Psalm 77. He almost sounds suspicious, doesn't he? I don't really believe that such a great man was truly questioning God so bluntly because he wasn't sure if God had his best interest in mind. I think that David penned these words as a way to visualize his pain.

Maybe you've been there. You do not mean to question God, and you probably wish you could take back a few words. Your heart is just so full of anguish and suffering that you have to let it out somehow. The best thing to do when these kinds of irrational thoughts possess your soul is to ask God for patience. Psalm 37:7 pleads with us to *"Rest in the LORD, and wait patiently for him...."* Romans 12:12 reads, *"Rejoicing in hope; patient in tribulation; continuing instant in prayer."*

We have to maintain a calm and rational state while we are dealing with the difficulty that presents itself to us at the moment. This calming affect can only flood our souls through the peace that God alone can provide. God gives us the recipe for calming our hearts and our minds in His Word. *"Be careful for nothing; but in every thing by prayer and supplication with thanksgiving let your requests be made known unto God. And the peace of God, which passeth all understanding, shall keep your hearts and minds through Christ Jesus."* (Philippians 4:6, 7)

The word "shall" in verse seven means that God promises **without fail** to give us a peace which passeth all understanding, and He will keep our hearts and mind. The answer to our searching and our wondering is to be found always on our knees in a humble submission to God and His master plan for our life. *"But the God of all grace, who hath called us unto his eternal glory by Christ Jesus, after that ye have suffered a while, make you perfect, stablish, strengthen, settle you."* (I Peter 5:10) The God of all grace, during your time of pain, will stablish, strengthen, and settle you.

You May Never Know Why

That's a depressing thought, isn't it? I'm sorry. Depressing my reader is very much not my intention, but I must also be truthful. The bottom line is that God doesn't owe anyone an explanation, and there are times when He chooses not to give one. The Bible never records Adam and Eve's finding out why God allowed one of their sons to be murdered. Conversely, God chose to allow Paul to understand exactly why he was being afflicted. II Corinthians 12:7 explains why Paul was given his hardship. *"And lest I should be exalted above measure through the abundance of the revelations, there was given to me a thorn in the flesh, the messenger of Satan to buffet me, lest I should be exalted above measure."* It's clear that Paul understood that he was given a physical limitation so that he would not be exalted in the eyes of men, thereby potentially jeopardizing Paul's humble spirit. Why did God explain Paul's affliction but not inform Adam and Eve as to why their son was allowed to die? The simple answer is that I don't know. But again, we can look to the Word of God and see that it is not up to us to understand.

Over and over again, the Bible reminds us that God is sovereign and just. That He doesn't reveal to us His reasons for certain decisions doesn't mean that He doesn't have very good ones. Deuteronomy 29:29 explains, *"The secret things belong unto the LORD our God: but those things that are revealed belong unto us and to our children for ever, that we may do all the words of this law."* The secret things belong to the Lord. We must accept that truth by faith in order to please God with our lives. *"But without faith it is impossible to please him: for he that cometh to God must believe that he is, and that he is a rewarder of them that diligently seek him."* (Hebrews 11:6)

Who can know the mind of God? Romans 11:33-36 gives the answer. *"O the depth of the riches both of the wisdom and knowledge of God! how unsearchable are his judgments, and his ways past finding out! [34]For who hath known the mind of the Lord? or who hath been his counseller? [35]Or who hath first given to him, and it shall be recompensed unto him again? [36]For of him, and through him, and to him, are all things: to whom be glory for ever. Amen."*

The answer is that it is impossible for our finite mind to comprehend the reasoning of an infinite Creator. Avail yourself of the peace that Christ is more than willing to give to each and every one of us. Continually remind yourself that just because God doesn't reveal to you His plans and designs, this lack of revelation doesn't mean that He hasn't carefully mapped out every stage of your life in His overwhelming love and unfailing care. If we are able to trust God completely and have faith in His ability to unfold our life exactly how it should be unfolded, there is some very exciting and comforting news on the horizon!

God Has a Reason

"And it came to pass, as we went to prayer, a certain damsel possessed with a spirit of divination met us, which brought her masters much gain by soothsaying: [17]The same followed Paul and us, and cried, saying, These men are the servants of the most high God, which shew unto us the way of salvation. [18]And this did she many days. But Paul, being grieved, turned and said to the spirit, I command thee in the name of Jesus Christ to come out of her. And he came out the same hour. [19]And when her masters saw that the hope of their gains was gone, they caught Paul and Silas, and drew them into the marketplace unto the rulers, [20]And brought them to the magistrates, saying, These men, being Jews, do exceedingly trouble our city, [21]And teach customs, which are not lawful for us to receive, neither to observe, being Romans. [22]And the multitude rose up together against them: and the magistrates rent off their clothes, and commanded to beat them. [23]And when they had laid many stripes upon them, they cast them into prison, charging the jailor to keep them safely: [24]Who, having received such a charge, thrust them into the inner prison, and made their feet fast in the stocks. [25]And at midnight Paul and Silas prayed, and sang praises unto God: and the prisoners heard them. [26]And suddenly there was a great earthquake, so that the foundations of the prison were shaken: and immediately all the doors were opened, and every one's bands were loosed. [27]And the keeper of the prison awaking out of his sleep, and seeing the prison doors open, he drew out his sword, and would have killed himself, supposing that the prisoners had been fled. [28]But Paul cried with a loud voice, saying, Do thyself no harm: for we are all here. [29]Then he called for a light, and sprang in, and came trembling, and fell down before Paul and Silas, [30]And brought them out, and said, Sirs, what must I do to be saved? [31]And they said, Believe on the Lord Jesus Christ, and thou shalt be saved, and thy house. [32]And they spake unto him the word of the Lord, and to all that were in his house. [33]And he took them the same hour of the night, and washed their stripes; and was baptized, he and *all his, straightway.* [34]*And when he had brought them into his house, he set meat before them, and rejoiced, believing in God with all his house."* (Acts 16:16-34)

This Scripture passage reveals a beautiful picture of two Christians who endured hardship with a joyous spirit because they possessed the confidence that God would not bring them through a trial without a wondrous purpose. Paul and Silas had done absolutely nothing wrong to deserve the suffering that they endured. In fact, they had performed a miracle! They released a young girl from demon possession as well as slave-like employment. Next, Paul and Silas were persecuted without any semblance of a fair trial. They were never given the opportunity to speak for themselves in an effort to refute the erroneous charges that were being attached to their name. These men of God who were simply trying to share the Gospel with a city were beaten and cast into an inner prison. Theirs was certainly a situation where practically anyone would have looked toward Heaven with disagreeing and angered eyes. But instead, Paul and Silas reacted to their predicament by praying and singing praises to God. Wow! In the middle of the night, sore from being physically abused and trapped in a prison because of a false accusation, they sang. And they didn't just sing anything; they sang praises to God!

How did these men manage to maintain such an optimistic and upbeat persona while in such dire circumstances? I would contend that they possessed such an amazing attitude because they knew enough about God to understand that He was about to do something great. Paul especially was a man well-acquainted with God's ability to take a terrible situation and bring about wondrous accomplishments for the kingdom of Heaven.

In II Corinthians 11:24-27 Paul listed just a few of the hardships that God had brought him through. *"Of the Jews five times received I forty stripes save one.* [25]*Thrice was I beaten with rods, once was I stoned, thrice I suffered shipwreck, a night and a day I have been in the deep;* [26]*In journeyings often, in perils of waters, in perils of robbers, in perils by mine own countrymen, in perils by the heathen, in perils in the city, in perils in the wilderness, in perils in the sea, in perils among false brethren;* [27]*In weariness and painfulness, in watchings often, in hunger and thirst, in fastings often, in cold and nakedness."*

Paul had been through the fire before, and he had seen God's provision and purpose. Paul and Silas had the faith in Christ to believe that He would perform a great work through their captivity. Guess what? They were right! God performed quite a dynamic and magnificent miracle that resulted in the freeing of Paul and Silas. Much more important than their release, however, was their opportunity to lead the jailor and his family to a saving knowledge of Jesus Christ! Luke 15:7 says, *"I say unto you, that likewise joy shall be in heaven over one sinner that repenteth, more than over ninety and nine just persons, which need no repentance."* Through the lens of Heaven, the salvation of the jailor was so much more imperative than the release of Paul and Silas. It sounds like Paul and Silas got "used," doesn't it? I don't think they cared. Why? They had so much assurance that there was a reason behind their trial that they were actually expecting and looking for the purpose.

Notice that when the prison doors opened, Paul and Silas didn't race out to freedom. They stayed behind. I believe that they realized that their deliverance was not all that God wanted to accomplish through the situation. He also wanted to save the jailor and his family. Paul and Silas potentially jeopardized their own liberty in order to ensure that God's full purpose for their circumstance had been completed. They knew God had a reason, and they didn't want to miss out on an opportunity to fulfill the will of God for their life!

Do we have that kind of faith? Do we so much trust the fact that God has a reason that we would potentially prolong our pain in order to accomplish His purposes? That's a tough one, isn't it? That's really what it comes down to with this question of "Why?"

- How much do I trust God?
- How much do I accept that He is in complete control of the "ins and outs" of my life?
- Am I okay with the fact that I don't get to call the shots?
- Am I satisfied if God never decides to reveal His reasoning to me?

I think that if we could honestly answer those questions, then we would discover the answer to the unavoidable question "Why?" If we are able to reach the point where we are content with God's being in control, then we won't be nearly as concerned with why the storms of life rage around us. Paul and Silas sang praises during their imprisonment because they were not the least bit concerned about the outcome of their challenge. That's how much they trusted that God knew what He was doing and would use their burden in a marvelous way! Can we say the same about the pain we have had or maybe are currently experiencing? If we can, then we know God has a reason, and we don't have to know "Why?" anymore.

When I think about this principle of God's having a reason behind every circumstance He brings into our life, I am again reminded of the miraculous story of Shadrach, Meshach, and Abednego and some remarkable truths about God's always having a reason for our trials.

"Now if ye be ready that at what time ye hear the sound of the cornet, flute, harp, sackbut, psaltery, and dulcimer, and all kinds of musick, ye fall down and worship the image which I have made; well: but if ye worship not, ye shall be cast the same hour into the midst of a burning fiery furnace; and who is that God that shall deliver you out of my hands? [16]Shadrach, Meshach, and Abednego, answered and said to the king, O Nebuchadnezzar, we are not careful to answer thee in this matter. [17]If it be so, our God whom we serve is able to deliver us from the burning fiery furnace, and he will deliver us out of thine hand, O king. [18]But if not, be it known unto thee, O king, that we will not serve thy gods, nor worship the golden image which thou hast set up. [19]Then was Nebuchadnezzar full of fury, and the form of his visage was changed against Shadrach, Meshach, and Abednego: therefore he spake, and commanded that they should heat the furnace one seven times more than it was wont to be heated. [20]And he commanded the most mighty men that were in his army to bind Shadrach, Meshach, and Abednego, and to cast them into the burning fiery furnace. [21]Then these men were bound in their coats, their hosen, and their hats, and their other garments, and were cast into the midst of the burn-

ing fiery furnace. ²²*Therefore because the king's commandment was urgent, and the furnace exceeding hot, the flame of the fire slew those men that took up Shadrach, Meshach, and Abednego.* ²³*And these three men, Shadrach, Meshach, and Abednego, fell down bound into the midst of the burning fiery furnace.* ²⁴*Then Nebuchadnezzar the king was astonied, and rose up in haste, and spake, and said unto his counsellors, Did not we cast three men bound into the midst of the fire? They answered and said unto the king, True, O king.* ²⁵*He answered and said, Lo, I see four men loose, walking in the midst of the fire, and they have no hurt; and the form of the fourth is like the Son of God.* ²⁶*Then Nebuchadnezzar came near to the mouth of the burning fiery furnace, and spake, and said, Shadrach, Meshach, and Abednego, ye servants of the most high God, come forth, and come hither. Then Shadrach, Meshach, and Abednego, came forth of the midst of the fire.* ²⁷*And the princes, governors, and captains, and the king's counsellors, being gathered together, saw these men, upon whose bodies the fire had no power, nor was an hair of their head singed, neither were their coats changed, nor the smell of fire had passed on them.* ²⁸*Then Nebuchadnezzar spake, and said, Blessed be the God of Shadrach, Meshach, and Abednego, who hath sent his angel, and delivered his servants that trusted in him, and have changed the king's word, and yielded their bodies, that they might not serve nor worship any god, except their own God.* ²⁹*Therefore I make a decree, That every people, nation, and language, which speak anything amiss against the God of Shadrach, Meshach, and Abednego, shall be cut in pieces, and their houses shall be made a dunghill: because there is no other God that can deliver after this sort.* ³⁰*Then the king promoted Shadrach, Meshach, and Abednego, in the province of Babylon."* (Daniel 3:15-30)

Believe in God's Provision

This portion of Scripture reveals the firm belief of Shadrach, Meshach, and Abednego in God's ability to care for His children. The three Hebrew children took a very aggressive tone with the king who had just threatened to burn them alive! They declared confidently that they didn't have to hesitate or contemplate because they were fully assured that God would rescue them. Do we have that same faith in our Saviour? When a burden lands on our shoulders, do we look at the circumstances and say, "...*we are not careful to answer thee in this matter. If it be so, our God whom we serve is able to deliver us...*"? Look back at your life, my friend. Hasn't God moved mountains for you before? Hasn't He done the impossible? He has in mine. Throughout this book, I will be sharing many of the impossibilities that God has made possible for me. How do we so quickly lose sight of His goodness? He Who has never failed us in the past is worthy to be trusted to never let us down in the present or future as well.

Believe in God's Providence

Shadrach, Meshach, and Abednego knew that God could deliver them; yet they also knew that even if He chose not to save them, He would have a reason for that decision as well. Thank God for such a remarkable display of faith by these men of God! *"But if not, be it known unto thee, O king, that we will not serve thy gods, nor worship the golden image which thou hast set up."* Not only did they proudly declare the power of God to save them, but they also explained the providence of the Almighty and His right NOT to save them if He so chose.

How many of us, when staring death in the eyes, would have the courage to say, "If God doesn't save me, that's okay too. He's in control. I will not stop doing right no matter what"? My point is this: Shadrach, Meshach, and Abednego didn't cower in fear and cry out, "Why?" No, the Bible never records their asking why. The Bible never records their questioning or wondering. The Bible records only their confidence in God's protection and providence.

There is much that a Christian can learn and apply to his life from the faith of these three Jewish rulers. Sometimes I believe we make the mistake of viewing great stories in the Bible like this one from a "finished" perspective. We look at how the story ended, and we suddenly paint a rosy picture of the events.

When we think about the story of Shadrach, Meshach, and Abednego, we are sometimes tempted to jump right to the point where the Son of God visibly appears in the fiery furnace. But take note that these three Jews couldn't see God when Nebuchadnezzar said, *"...but if ye worship not, ye shall be cast the same hour into the midst of a burning fiery furnace; and who is that God that shall deliver you out of my hands?"* It took more than just a grain of mustard seed worth of faith to stare down the king after a threat like that one!

Jesus didn't show up in a tangible, visible way until they were all the way IN the fire. The boldness of these three men should be a tremendous encouragement to every Christian. If Shadrach, Meshach, and Abednego can face the trial of being thrown into a burning fiery furnace, then I can handle the pathetic arthritis that God has given to me! If these men can be tied up and thrown into the midst of a fire without verbally questioning God one time, then we can do it as well!

Believe in God's Purpose for the Fire

Guess what? God brought these three young people through a tremendous trial and burden, and He had great reason for it. The whole time God was completely conscious of exactly what He intended to accomplish through the fire! We don't have to know why as long as we know Who is in control! So why were Shadrach, Meshach, and Abednego thrown into the fire? Most likely God had a plethora of reasons for the trial of these three young men, but He took the time to record a few specifics that would have never happened without these Hebrew young men's enduring the trial of their life.

1. **The king would not have seen God.** *"Then Nebuchadnezzar the king was astonied, and rose up in haste, and spake, and said unto his counsellers, Did not we cast three men bound into the midst of the fire? They answered and said unto the king, True, O king. He answered and said, Lo, I see four men loose, walking in the midst of the fire, and they have no hurt; and the form of the fourth is like the Son of God."* (Daniel 3:24, 25) Until he had thrown Shadrach, Meshach, and Abednego into the fire, Nebuchadnezzar was unable to see the Son of God. Likewise, sometimes

God needs us to jump into a fire so that someone looking on can see Him!

One of the greatest joys of my life has been a few times when a person has walked up to me and expressed that they could see Jesus shining through my life. What a blessing! What a privilege! That kind of compliment really should fill our hearts with joy. The thought that quite possibly the suffering that we are currently enduring could be a window for someone to catch a glimpse of Jesus Christ is exciting.

I Peter 4:13 says, *"But rejoice, inasmuch as ye are partakers of Christ's sufferings; that, when his glory shall be revealed, ye may be glad also with exceeding joy."* The Bible commands that we rejoice in our suffering because there will come a time *"when his glory shall be revealed."* And when that glory is allowed to be revealed in us, that should bring us *"exceeding joy"*! However, before we can experience that great joy, we must get in the fire. I feel sure that Shadrach, Meshach, and Abednego were happy that they helped Nebuchadnezzar see the Son of God, but that would have never happened if these three Hebrew rulers hadn't been put in the burning furnace. God had a reason!

2. **The king would not have been astonished.** *"Then Nebuchadnezzar the king was astonied...."* (Daniel 3:24) It's very awesome when someone's going through a very painful experience with grace and strength causes the people around them to begin to wonder. The people privileged to look on begin to wonder, "What does that person have that allows him to accept his burden so easily?" I believe that's what Nebuchadnezzar was wondering. "How were these three men not being consumed in the fire?" His questioning prompted him to go to the mouth of the fire and look for himself. The fiery trial of Shadrach, Meshach, and Abednego drove the king to astonishment and eventually to God.

Seemingly, one of the most popular reasons behind our earthly suffering is our loving Saviour's need to draw to Him many of the wandering and straying souls who have lost all concept of Him or His goodness. So He finds it necessary to send a "wake-up" call, if you will. Apparently seeing four men walking around in a fire without even so much as smelling like smoke was all the "wake-up" call that Nebuchadnezzar needed! The king would have never been astonished or driven to God, however, without Shadrach, Meshach, and Abednego's getting into the inferno. God had a reason!

3.   **The kingdom would have never turned to God.** *"Therefore I make a decree, That every people, nation, and language, which speak anything amiss against the God of Shadrach, Meshach, and Abednego, shall be cut in pieces, and their houses shall be made a dunghill: because there is no other God that can deliver after this sort."* (Daniel 3:29) In this verse the king who just moments ago was forcing his entire kingdom to worship a graven image of himself is now decreeing that if anyone speaks ill of the One and only true God, he will be cut in pieces! Quite a turnaround! I really don't think many occurrences or happenings would have provoked such a drastic change in the life of the king. It just so happens that God had a plan that He knew would work! He knew His plan would turn the kingdom back to Him. In order for that plan to be effective, though, Shadrach, Meshach, and Abednego had to do their part.

God also has a marvelous and sure-fire plan that He would love to execute through our lives as well, but just like the three Hebrew rulers—we must to do our part. I know that through my tumors, God has a plan. I know that through my arthritis, God has a reason. I know that through my uveitis, God has a purpose. My challenge is to allow myself to be put in the fire so that the Son of Man can show up and turn the kingdom back to Him. By the way, that's your challenge as well.

God had so many valid reasons for allowing Shadrach, Meshach, and Abednego to go through their challenge outlined in Daniel chapter three. God wants to accomplish wondrous things through the challenges of our life as well. We waste a lot of time trying to figure out why we are going through a hardship when we should be trying to figure out what God wants to do with us or through us. As we have seen, there really is a reason behind whatever happens to us. God decides and approves everything that occurs in our life, and He means it for our good or for the good of others. The burdens that we carry and the trials that we endure are necessary in order to perform the works that God knows must be done.

The heartbreaking and heartwarming story of the potter and the clay found in the book of Jeremiah sums up why we are afflicted the way we are.

> "*The word which came to Jeremiah from the LORD, saying, ²Arise, and go down to the potter's house, and there I will cause thee to hear my words. ³Then I went down to the potter's house, and, behold, he wrought a work on the wheels. ⁴And the vessel that he made of clay was marred in the hand of the potter: so he made it again another vessel, as seemed good to the potter to make it.*"

(Jeremiah 18:1-4)

You've heard it before—a Christian is the marred clay in the awesome hand of his Creator. God has a bold and incredible plan for our life, but we are marred. These blemishes must be purified before a Christian can truly succeed to the level that He desires. So there are times when the Potter has to sit at His wheel and make His child *"again another vessel."* This purification process is painful, and it's scary. But it's worth it in the end.

Job 23:10 says, "*...when he hath tried me, I shall come forth as gold.*" I am sure that Paul and Silas would say it was worth the beatings and imprisonment so the jailor and his family could accept Christ as their Saviour. I'm sure the three Hebrew rulers would say it was worth the fiery furnace so that the king could see God, be astonished, and turn the kingdom back to God. And whether or not we can see it now, God's plan is worth whatever we have been through, too. It's worth the pain. It's worth the suffering. It's worth the tears. It's worth it because there is a masterful Potter Who is lovingly and carefully making His child into a vessel as seems good to Him to make. With His help, let's stop asking "Why?" and let's start trusting that "*...he which hath begun a good work in you will perform it until the day of Jesus Christ.*" (Philippians 1:6)

It occurs to me as I finish this chapter why I can no longer play basketball. It's not because of my arthritis and physical limitations. If I still played basketball, though, much of my time would be filled up with practices, travel, and games. I doubt I would have time to be writing this book. That's why God took basketball away from me; it was a marred part of me that had to go in order to make time to accomplish a much more important work for His honor and glory. That's why.

CHAPTER THREE

LET IT GO

Overcoming Bitterness and Anger

I don't have a clue what you have been through in life. That's pretty obvious, right? More than likely, I have never met you; therefore, there is no way for me to be acquainted with the trials and troubles that you have endured. No doubt some people who have experienced what the world would commonly consider horrible and devastating circumstances will pick up this book. I am sure some, if not many, of those who will read this book have experienced far worse than I have ever dreamed of in my life. Probably there are those who have been molested and abused. There are those who have been faced with a debilitating and possibly terminal disease. Some may have been in valleys of depression that most would be unable to comprehend. As diverse as most of my readers' backgrounds will be, I imagine not one of them has been thrown into a pit, sold into slavery by his family, falsely accused of sexual immorality, and thrown into prison without a trial. I am just hazarding a guess that those particular circumstances have never happened to anyone in this day and age—certainly not all of them.

These unique circumstances paint a terrible life, don't they? Getting thrown into a pit would ruin a person's day. Being sold into slavery by the people who are supposed to love and protect you would hurt. Being falsely accused of a despicable, horrible sin would be difficult. Getting tossed into prison when you are guilty of nothing would be rough. Put these hurts all together, and it just seems like too much to bear, doesn't it? Who wants to live that life? I hate to even think about it, but it's no secret that hundreds of people commit suicide every year over much less than these circumstances. One man, however, did indeed go through all of these circumstances before he was even 30 years of age. Of course I am referring to Joseph in the Old Testament.

Genesis 37:23, 24

"And it came to pass, when Joseph was come unto his brethren, that they stript Joseph out of his coat, his coat of many colours that was on him; [24]And they took him, and cast him into a pit: and the pit was empty, there was no water in it."

Genesis 37:27, 28

"Come, and let us sell him to the Ishmeelites, and let not our hand be upon him; for he is our brother and our flesh. And his brethren were content. [28]Then there passed by Midianites merchantmen; and they drew and lifted up Joseph out of the pit, and sold Joseph to the Ishmeelites for twenty pieces of silver: and they brought Joseph into Egypt."

Genesis 39:7-20

"And it came to pass after these things, that his master's wife cast her eyes upon Joseph; and she said, Lie with me. [8]But he refused, and said unto his master's wife, Behold, my master wotteth not what is with me in the house, and he hath committed all that he hath to my hand; [9]There is none greater in this house than I; neither hath he kept back any thing from me but thee, because thou art his wife: how then can I do this great wickedness, and sin against God? [10]And it came to pass, as she spake to Joseph day by day, that he hearkened not unto her, to lie by her, or to be with her. [11]And it came to pass about this time, that Joseph went into the house to do his business; and there was none of the men of the house there within. [12]And she caught him by his garment, saying, Lie with me: and he left his garment in her hand, and fled, and got him out. [13]And it came to pass, when she saw that he had left his garment in her hand, and was fled forth, [14]That she called unto the men of her house, and spake unto them, saying, See, he hath brought in an Hebrew unto us to mock us; he came in unto me to lie with me, and I cried with a loud voice: [15]And it came to pass, when he heard that I lifted up my voice and cried, that he left his garment with me, and fled, and got him out. [16]And she laid up his garment by her, until his lord came home. [17]And she spake unto him according to these words, saying, The Hebrew *servant, which thou hast brought unto us, came in unto me to mock me:* [18]*And it came to pass, as I lifted up my voice and cried, that he left his garment with me, and fled out.* [19]*And it came to pass, when his master heard the words of his wife, which she spake unto him, saying, After this manner did thy servant to me; that his wrath was kindled.* [20]*And Joseph's master took him, and put him in the prison, a place where the king's prisoners were bound: and he was there in the prison."*

Yes, all this really did all happen to one man. As I compare my life to Joseph's, I must admit that my tumors, arthritis, eye problems, and pain really begin to look rather pathetic. Let me say though, if I had been Joseph, I think I would have been quite upset. Let me rephrase: I'd basically be furious. What did Joseph do anyway? Why him? Why did his life have to be so miserable? Talk about having the world turn against you! I think I would have been very angry and very bitter. So Joseph was angry and bitter, right? He resented and despised God, right? Well, actually no. In fact, never once did Joseph complain about his situation. That's amazing! To go through everything that Joseph did and not cultivate a bitter or malicious spirit is remarkable. In this chapter I want to examine how Joseph was able to keep his heart of contentment in spite of the tremendous darkness of his life. An examination of Joseph's life will teach how to put away any bitterness or anger that may be poisoning one's heart.

Just like I don't know what you may suffer from, neither do I know if you have trouble controlling your spirit toward God and others. But even if you are the happiest and most upbeat person in the world, it's still a struggle. It's a constant battle to make sure that our heart stays right while it seems like our surrounding world crashes in upon our life. It is absolutely critical, however, that we put away any bitterness from our soul in order to accept the difficulties that God has placed into our life. If we spend our life handcuffed by the past and the emotions of the present, we completely forfeit the happiness and productivity that God would love to bring to us. We must first address the problems that present themselves when we refuse to let go of the pain and bitterness that may be built up in our hearts.

Bitterness Adds to Our Problems

Have you ever watched someone who is in a bad position absolutely making matters worse for himself? My dad often tells stories about his grandmother. My great-grandmother was a sweet Christian lady, but for some unknown reason she just couldn't allow herself to be happy in life. My dad says that if she even thought she was going to have a good day, she would start throwing pots and pans across the kitchen and intentionally break things so that she would have something about which to be upset. That's just crazy, isn't it? She just had to compound her problems and elongate her difficulties. I know she was a dear lady, and I can't wait to meet her in Heaven one day, but her behavior was simply illogical and inexplicable!

However, what we have to realize is that we do the exact same thing when we allow bitterness and anger to creep into our souls. Just like my great-grandmother, who always made matters worse, some people take their already painful situation and add to their misery. Bitterness has never made a sick child well. Anger has never brought a loved one back to God. Malice toward God has never reversed the past. It just doesn't work. All these negative emotions do is multiply one's current pain and increase the suffering.

For example, if I were to become angry and bitter toward God for the physical limitations that He has placed upon me, my feelings would not do a single thing to make my joints bend or stop hurting. All those feelings would do is add emotional and spiritual pain to my physical problems. Being angry and bitter is definitely not in my best interest, is it? It just does not make sense. Yet it appears that many people allow themselves to be trapped by these feelings. I have been trapped myself. I'm ashamed to admit it, but I would be lying if I said that I was never frustrated and bitter over the struggles with which I am faced on a day-to-day basis. We have to be so careful because bitterness not only adds to our problems, but it also limits the blessings that God would love to produce from our pain.

Bitterness Robs Us of Our Productivity

This, I believe, is perhaps the most severe threat that anger and bitterness poses to our life, soul, and heart. When we allow ourselves to be transfixed upon the negative emotions that grip our heart, we rob ourselves and the others that God would like to help through our suffering. As long as we are still upset about the burden or trial that we have dealt with in the past or are currently dealing with in the present, we will never be able to take the next steps of embracing and using our difficulties for the glory of God. If you hate your burden or limitation, you will never be able to help someone else with that same problem. If you are angry about your weakness or suffering, you will never be able to experience the blessings that God has for your life.

If I were bitter about the circumstances in my life, I probably wouldn't be writing this book, would I? It's so imperative that we accept our pain by letting go of the bitterness and pain that fight to find a stronghold in our soul. There are several key steps that I believe we must take in order to free ourselves of the bondage of bitterness and anger.

Realize That Trouble Must Come

Life is made up of so many different facets, experiences, and events. Even at a young age, I am becoming increasingly aware of the Neapolitan nature of life. Every adult knows that in life he has to expect the bad with the good. Life is not unadulterated joy 24/7. It never has been; it never will be. It's just the natural way of life. The moment that the world or God seems to turn against us, the immediate temptation is to start losing focus of the fact that trouble must come. *"Then said his wife unto him, Dost thou still retain thine integrity? curse God, and die. But he said unto her, Thou speakest as one of the foolish women speaketh. What? Shall we receive good at the hand of God, and shall we not receive evil? In all this did not Job sin with his lips."* (Job 2:9, 10) Job makes a very wise observation in verse number ten. Job's wife was encouraging him to become bitter and angry because of the terrible tragedies that had just befallen him. However, Job realized that his wife was apparently blinded to the fact that bad has to be accepted along with the good. It is foolish not to. Job realized that he had received many blessings from God, and now he had to receive the negative circumstances as well.

It seems hard for people to accept this fact. We want life to be luxury and ease. If it were up to us, we would make sure that we bypassed every hardship, trial, and burden that could potentially come our way. But God, in His infinite wisdom and knowledge, knows what would become of us if we never had to fight. He knows what weak and helpless Christians we would become if we never had a battle to fight or a race to run.

Don't be surprised when the news of trouble reaches your ear. *"Beloved, think it not strange concerning the fiery trial which is to try you, as though some strange thing happened unto you."* (I Peter 4:12) I'm afraid that many people get so angry when the trials of life come along because they are just not expecting it. My dad often says, "If you haven't experienced a heartache yet, just keep breathing." His words are so true. You know they are, and I know they are. If you haven't experienced a serious and difficult set of circumstances, you will.

We all have to accept the trials that come into our life. I know it's difficult, but we have to allow God to revolutionize our thinking when it comes to life. We have to allow Him to help us accept the bad with the good. That's the first crucial step that we must take in overcoming bitterness and anger.

Realize That God's Blessings Outweigh Our Problems

Realizing that God's blessings will always outweigh our problems can be such a struggle to accept when we are in the midst of a storm, can't it? Trying to remind ourself that Christ gives us so many more blessings than He ever gives us trials can be tough to remember. You have no doubt been through a multitude of diverse burdens in your life. In a few hours of time, you could probably write down the major struggles that you have endured through the grace of God. You can number your trials, but according to Psalm 40:5 you can never, ever number the blessings and wonderful works of God. *"Many, O LORD my God, are thy wonderful works which thou hast done, and thy thoughts which are to us-ward: they cannot be reckoned up in order unto thee: if I would declare and speak of them, they are **more than can be numbered**."* God's blessings are more numerable than the sands of the sea and the stars of the sky. Ask the Lord to open your eyes and show you clearly all of the bountiful blessings that He showers upon you. Psalm 68:19 says, *"Blessed be the Lord, who daily loadeth us with benefits, even the God of our salvation. Selah."* People get so weighed down with the cares and tribulations of this world that they often seem to miss the load of benefits received from the hand of God on a daily basis. The air we breathe, our loved ones, our material possessions, and every other blessing in our life stems straight from the mercy and grace of our Lord Jesus Christ. The last part of Psalm 68:19 says, *"...even the God of our salvation."* Christians must live with a constant realization that we have a God Who has provided for our salvation. Salvation alone is such a blessing that it singlehandedly outweighs every other obstacle or difficulty or weakness in life. If Heaven were all that God ever gave us, it would by itself be enough to make life worth it.

Obviously, however, Heaven isn't all that we get out of the Christian life. Ask the Lord to help you to remember that the blessings and joys of life far outweigh the sorrows and heartache. Recognizing this truth is so important in overcoming bitterness and anger. If somebody hands you a $100 dollar bill, will you care if you have to pay a $10 parking ticket that day? You shouldn't. You still came out on top, $90 strong! I know it's hard for people to put this in perspective because the trial can be so dominating and consuming. But compared to the tremendous blessings that God pours upon us, our trial is like a silly $10 parking ticket. Psalm 103:2 declares, *"Bless the LORD, O my soul, and forget not all his benefits."*

Get Your Eyes Off Your Trouble

This principle follows closely along the lines of the previous idea for overcoming bitterness and anger. May I encourage you not just to remember all of the blessings of God but also to simply get your eyes off of your own trouble. People make a terrible mistake when they allow the difficulties of life to consume them. We've all watched people literally waste away under the pressure of a burden. Maybe you're doing the same thing right now with something with which you are struggling. We get so focused on the problems that we ignore every other aspect of life. I have seen mothers not take care of their children because they were so selfishly consumed with their own trouble. The consequences of too much focus on pain can be devastating. There is a secret to getting your eyes off of your own troubles. Stop looking at your own problems and focus on others. The world is full of people who have been through tremendous trials and tragedies; it's not just us. Everyone is suffering. *"For we know that the whole creation groaneth and travaileth in pain together...."* (Romans 8:22)

One of my favorite portions of Scripture is found in Hebrews chapter eleven. How inspirational and encouraging it is to read of the many people who have endured hardness and suffering with patience and joy!

"Who through faith subdued kingdoms, wrought righteousness, obtained promises, stopped the mouths of lions, [34]Quenched the violence of fire, escaped the edge of the sword, out of weakness were made strong, waxed valiant in fight, turned to flight the armies of the aliens. [35]Women received their dead raised to life again: and others were tortured, not accepting deliverance; that they might obtain a better resurrection: [36]And others had trial of cruel mockings and scourgings, yea, moreover of bonds and imprisonment: [37]They were stoned, they were sawn asunder, were tempted, were slain with the sword: they wandered about in sheepskins and goatskins; being destitute, afflicted, tormented; [38](Of whom the world was not worthy:) they wandered in deserts, and in mountains, and in dens and caves of the earth." (Hebrews 11:33-38)

When I read that passage of Scripture, I forget all about the pathetic problems with which I've dealt in my lifetime. It's words like "sawn asunder" that really make me understand that my situation could be worse! Sometimes I think it would really help us if we would just take a step back, stop thinking about our difficulties, look around us, and realize that so many people have gone through similar or more difficult hardships. It would be inappropriate for me to speak for you, but in my case, it helps me to look around and see the many other people who have suffered far worse than I have. Yes, my knees hurt. Yes, my eyesight is deplorable. Yes, I don't have my top teeth. And yes, I've had more surgeries than birthdays. Who cares? Compared to "sawn asunder," I've had it so easy! Even at my young age, I know so many people who have so many more hardships and so much more pain. And let me say that I'll take my physical problems over emotional, mental, and certainly spiritual problems any day of the week.

Look for the rainbow, my friend! Search for the silver lining. You might have to cope with a tragedy that seems staggering in magnitude, but until you've been cut in half...you have certainly had it better than some people! That's just the truth.

Genesis chapter 40 tells how Joseph handled the multitude of serious tribulations that God sent his way. A completely innocent Joseph sat in prison for crimes he did not commit. But instead of moaning in a corner cell about how horribly unfair his life was, the Bible records that Joseph was busy doing something else.

> *"And it came to pass after these things, that the butler of the king of Egypt and his baker had offended their lord the king of Egypt. ²And Pharaoh was wroth against two of his officers, against the chief of the butlers, and against the chief of the bakers. ³And he put them in ward in the house of the captain of the guard, into the prison, the place where Joseph was bound. ⁴And the captain of the guard charged Joseph with them and he served them: and they continued a season in ward."* (Genesis 40:1-4)

Two other prisoners were put in the same ward as Joseph by the pharaoh of Egypt. Joseph's interaction with the butler and baker did not involve whining or complaining about his difficult situation. No, instead Joseph served them, took care of them, and ministered to them. Part of the reason why Joseph was able to avoid bitterness and anger toward God and those who had hurt him was due to his ability to focus on the needs of others. With the Lord's help, may we do the same.

Realize God Has Not Abandoned You

> *"And **the Lord was with Joseph**, and he was a prosperous man; and he was in the house of his master the Egyptian."* (Genesis 39:2)

> *"But **the Lord was with Joseph**, and shewed him mercy, and gave him favour in the sight of the keeper of the prison."* (Genesis 39:21)

"*The keeper of the prison looked not to any thing that was under his hand; because the LORD was with him, and that which he did, the LORD made it to prosper.*" (Genesis 39:23)

In three separate verses, the Bible repeats the same mantra: the Lord was with Joseph. He was afflicted, desolate, and mistreated—but not alone! God allowed him to be sold into slavery and cast into prison, but He did not leave Joseph to fend for himself. God was right there with him through all of the trials. God made Joseph to prosper despite the enormous difficulties that Joseph was experiencing.

I believe, without a doubt, that Joseph was aware of the presence of God in his life. Joseph aptly avoided a bitter and angry spirit because he knew that God had not deserted him; rather, God was merely trying to accomplish a goal through Joseph's affliction.

God has not deserted you or me either. He's strengthening us, challenging us, and molding us, but He's not abandoning us. He won't. He can't. "*There shall not any man be able to stand before thee all the days of thy life: as I was with Moses, so I will be with thee: I will not fail thee, nor forsake thee.*" (Joshua 1:5)

Hebrews 13:5 reiterates, "*Let your conversation be without covetousness; and be content with such things as ye have: for he hath said, I will never leave thee, nor forsake thee.*" The Word of God gently and lovingly reminds the Christian to be content with the situations in which he finds himself because he can rest assured that God will never leave him on his own. Christian, don't be bitter. Turn to the loving Heavenly Father who stands next to you just waiting to envelope you in the warm and tender embrace that you need. "*Draw nigh to God, and he will draw nigh to you…*." (James 4:8) He's standing right by you waiting to wipe away your tears. Know that, believe that, and take advantage of that fact. The valleys of life are so dark that we must have His strength, or we really won't be able to make it. Don't leave Him because He hasn't left you.

> "*The LORD is my shepherd; I shall not want. ²He maketh me to lie down in green pastures: he leadeth me beside the still waters. ³He restoreth my soul: he leadeth me in the paths of righteousness for his name's sake. ⁴Yea, though I walk through the valley of the*

shadow of death, I will fear no evil: for thou art with me; thy rod and thy staff they comfort me. [5]Thou preparest a table before me in the presence of mine enemies: thou anointest my head with oil; my cup runneth over. [6]Surely goodness and mercy shall follow me all the days of my life: and I will dwell in the house of the Lord for ever." (Psalm 23)

Realize Your Affliction Is for Your Good

That's the trap that we fall into, isn't it? No matter how hard we might try to believe it or how many times we hear someone say it, we just don't accept the fact that our affliction is for our good. It's so difficult to realize that the reason why we suffer is that there is a greater good that must be served. We are human; therefore, our natural reactions tend to overwhelm our better judgment. This hijack of our emotions results in the bitterness that must be fought so fiercely. We blame God and put righteousness on our own personal judgment seat. We doubt God's goodness, forget His blessings, and zero in on what we perceive to be mistakes at His hand. "Why is He picking on me anyway?" "Why does He hate me?" We lose all rationale and logical faculties when we are so driven by the anger that Satan plants inside our heart.

Thankfully, God's servant Joseph was able to maintain a clear-headed and Christ-centered perspective on his suffering.

"And Joseph said unto his brethren, Come near to me, I pray you. And they came near. And he said, I am Joseph your brother, whom ye sold into Egypt. [5]Now therefore be not grieved, nor angry with yourselves, that ye sold me hither: for God did send me before you to preserve life. [6]For these two years hath the famine been in the land: and yet there are five years, in the which there shall neither be earing nor harvest. [7]And God sent me before you to preserve you a posterity in the earth, and to save your lives by a great deliverance. [8]So now it was not you that sent me hither, but God...."

(Genesis 45:4-8)

Joseph displayed such penetrating wisdom. He understood that it wasn't his brothers who placed him in his affliction; it was God. God sent him to Egypt because He had a miraculous plan and design for the life of Joseph. He needed Joseph to end up in Egypt and endure his suffering in order to save a multitude of lives! Within that plan of suffering came promotion for Joseph to a position of prominence in the kingdom. God didn't make a mistake or hate Joseph. God had a higher plan.

It's the same with us. God hasn't accidentally allowed your weakness and tribulation to enter your world. He hasn't afflicted you because He despises you and revels in your misery. He loves you more than you could ever understand, but He has a master plan that He must accomplish through you—for your good. Joseph is God's magnificent example of every attitude that every Christian must embody as he deals with difficulties. Joseph went so far as to name one of his sons "Ephraim" whose Biblical meaning is seen in Genesis 41:52. *"And the name of the second called he Ephraim: For God hath caused me to be **fruitful in the land of my affliction.***"

God wants to make every Christian fruitful in the land of his affliction as well. But in order for Him to do that, we must make sure we have the right attitude toward Him. He cannot help us if we possess bitter and hate-filled attitudes toward the One Who wants so desperately to be of assistance and aid. May we all take a cue from Joseph and recognize that our trials are truly for our good. *"But as for you, ye thought evil against me; **but God meant it unto good**, to bring to pass, as it is this day, to save much people alive."* (Genesis 50:20)

Forgive Those Who Have Hurt You

I love people. I promise I really do. However, I do find people are quite hilarious sometimes. Whenever my dad and I get roped into going shopping with my mom and sisters, the first thing we try to do is find a bench in an open area. If we are at a mall, we try to find the food court. Why? Because that is where we can watch the most people. Dad and I love to "people-watch." It's fantastic! I'm serious! Watching people is better than any television program any day of the week. It is seriously free entertainment. However, I must admit that if you sit and glance at the people walking by, what you see can really dampen your hopes and dreams for the human race in a hurry! My dad and I have watched some of the oddest, strangest, and downright weirdest people just by sitting in our local mall and observing. People watching can actually be scary sometimes! One thing that I have noticed about myself is that I am always drawn to whoever looks the most different from everyone else. If a person is wearing mismatched or out-of-style clothing, or seems just plain odd, I always find my eyes drawn toward that particular individual. Seemingly, most people just have a natural curiosity for the unusual, and many people consider those who have physical problems to be unusual. Furthermore, a large percentage of people seem to have a complete deficiency in tactfulness. I have noticed that when you put an overdeveloped curiosity level and a woeful lack of tact together, the results can be very interesting.

For example, I have had many complete strangers approach me and ask why I limp, why my wrists don't move, why I can't jump, why my knees barely bend, and the list could go on and on. Now honestly, I understand that some people are genuinely compassionate, which is why I endeavor never to be rude when I am approached this way, but in truth, my medical history is really not a complete stranger's business! Still I am amazed at how I am stopped on a semi-regular basis. People in restaurants, stores, and parking lots just stop me and start asking questions. What possesses people to do that?

I'm sure you have also had people who are not bold enough to ask you what's wrong, so they just stare like you are the very first human they've ever seen. Either way, these kinds of situations are never comfortable for the one being scrutinized. As a Christian, I am called to be patient and longsuffering when it comes to dealing with this kind of behavior from other people, but let's be honest…that's not always easy. It's awkward and it's uncomfortable, and the truth is, I don't like it. I'd be lying if I told you I didn't mind.

And of course, I have had some people make downright nasty and insulting remarks about my physical difficulties. It happens; that's reality. More than likely, you've had similar situations come into your life. It hurts, doesn't it? Of course it does. I've had situations where I have had to just walk away from people who have directly and purposefully said insensitive things. Unfortunately, even very close friends of mine have from time to time said some really unwise and painful things, and from those people, it hurts the most. I have learned I must be so careful because these feelings of frustration are the mother of a lifetime ruined by bitterness.

The key to avoiding bitterness when others have done us wrong and added to our pain is obviously forgiveness. So much easier said than done, right? I know. In my own situation, it is most likely easier for me to forgive than you. Yes, I have gotten angry and upset from time to time, but it's not that difficult to forgive someone for just being ignorant. Maybe you've had people perpetrate far worse acts against you.

As I write this chapter, I'm thinking of two young people whom I know who, sadly, were abused and molested when they were young. I cannot begin to comprehend or understand that kind of pain. I can't comprehend the scars with which these wonderful friends of mine have to cope for the rest of their life. My heart breaks every time I think of their past. But more than just sadness, I also feel anger for them. When I think about the strong emotions that I feel toward those who hurt my friends, I wonder how deeply my friends must despise their abusers? How do they forgive the people who treated them so despicably? I cannot imagine theirs is an easy or simple process.

Forgiveness is one of the most basic, yet seemingly most complicated and complex teachings in the Word of God. I will not pretend that I can give you the secret to being able to willingly and permanently forgive those who have brought hurt to your life. Only God can. I would encourage you, though, to keep in mind the standard of forgiveness that is taught in the Bible. May I point you to the example of forgiveness that we are to emulate? *"And be ye kind one to another, tenderhearted, forgiving one another, even as God for Christ's sake hath forgiven you."* (Ephesians 4:32)

Think for a minute about all of the different ways that we have grieved God. Think of the many times we've turned our back on Him, sinned against Him, and broken His heart. Now think about the composite of all of mankind and the trespasses that mankind as a whole has committed against our Creator. God forgave mankind for all of that!

God is willing to cast every bit of that sin behind Him—never to remember it again.

Ephesians teaches that the Christian has the capacity to forgive others just as God forgave. That's a high standard, I know. In fact, it's the highest standard conceivable. But without the willingness to forgive those who have brought hurt to our lives, we will never be able to be delivered from the emotional and spiritual bondage of bitterness and anger. *"And they stoned Stephen, calling upon God, and saying, Lord Jesus, receive my spirit. And he kneeled down, and cried with a loud voice, **Lord, lay not this sin to their charge.** And when he had said this, he fell asleep."* (Acts 7:59, 60) Like Stephen, we must offer forgiveness.

We Must Let Go of the Past

Often, one of the hardest things to do is let go of a burden when it is time to move on with our lives. At first you may think to yourself, "No, it's not. I want to move on. I don't have any problem with being delivered from my troubles!" Wait! I didn't say, "It's hard to move on when you get delivered from your troubles." I said, "It's hard to move on when it's time." I have learned that it is often time to move on from a trial before we get delivered. Let me attempt to explain what I mean with a personal example. I have had polyarticular juvenile rheumatoid arthritis since 1991. God has not chosen to deliver me from this disease. But a long time ago, I felt the strong call from God that it was time to move on.

What do I mean by "moving on"? That's a fair question. What I mean is that I felt strongly that my arthritis was not supposed to define me. It wasn't supposed to be what characterized my life. When people think "Dave McCroskey," I don't want them to think "arthritis." I don't want them to think of me as handicapped or disabled at all. I've fiercely fought those labels throughout my life. I have had doctors through the years who have tried to make me use a handicapped parking pass, and I have refused every time. I won't take one because I don't need one. When people think of me, I want them to think of someone who loves God and lives to encourage others. You see, God hasn't delivered me from my arthritis, but neither is my arthritis supposed to define me. I've moved on. I have literally had days when my arthritis doesn't ever enter my mind. Of course I'm conscious of the fact that I'm in pain and am physically limited, but I don't dwell on it. I don't think about it. It's a part of me, but it's not **me**.

There are burdens and trials that you may be holding on to right now. Maybe it's a tragedy that you haven't gotten over. Maybe it's a trial that you still worry about and fret over even though it's in the past. The problem is that when we allow our mind to fester and mull over what has happened in the past, we open the door to bitterness in our life. Paul gives great advice in Philippians chapter three for anyone who is having a hard time moving on from a painful experience in the past. *"Brethren, I count not myself to have apprehended: but this one thing I do, **forgetting those things which are behind**, and reaching forth unto those things which are before. I press toward the mark for the prize of the high calling of God in Christ Jesus."* (Philippians 3:13, 14)

The Apostle Paul implores us to forget those things that are behind, and Paul makes clear the reason why we must forget about the past. We must free ourselves from the past, or we can never reach forth toward those things which are before. We can never press toward the mark until we decide, with God's help, to move on from the past!

Here's the key, my friend. Until we accept the trials and difficulties of our life, we can never be the useful and productive Christian that God so desperately desires for us to become. There's a prize that He wants us to win. There's a life He wants us to touch. There's a mission He needs us to accomplish. But we will never be able to do that until we accept the difficulties that God has given us and get over the bitterness and anger that so easily arrest us.

We all have cups that God has given us. And whether we know why or whether we don't understand at all, we all have a burden to bear in life. We all have pain. We all experience suffering. Those are the facts of life. We have two options when considering how to deal with the trouble.

Option Number One

We can become bitter, angry, and completely useless to God and His plan for our life through our suffering.

Option Number Two

We can accept our pain as the will of God for our life and absolutely begin to revolutionize our thought process through the grace and strength of Christ.

There is so much more than just accepting our suffering, though. We still have the steps of embracing and then using our troubles as well. But we can never get to those steps until we take the first one. Accept what God has given to you! You cannot change it. You can't wave a magic wand and make it all disappear. It doesn't work that way. It never will. Take the first step of accepting your God-given difficulties so that you can then fall on your knees and ask Him to show you the next step that He would have you to take. And by all means, *"Let all bitterness, and wrath, and anger, and clamour, and evil speaking, be put away from you, with all malice."* (Ephesians 4:31) Your bitterness will never change anything about your life. All it accomplishes is to make your situation worse and paralyze your usefulness for God. I'm begging you…let it go.

*"All the world is full of suffering.
It is also full of overcoming."*

– Helen Keller

CHAPTER FOUR

FALLING IN LOVE

Embracing Your Difficulties

I suppose you could say it's a classic love story. He grew in up southern Montgomery, Alabama. She lived out her childhood in urban Minneapolis, Minnesota. For any who are geographically challenged, Montgomery and Minneapolis aren't exactly in the same zip code region. In fact, some would argue that Montgomery and Minneapolis aren't even in the same country! But distance wasn't a problem for God. He was able to lead both of them to the exact same college in the exact same year. The first week of college they met each other, and the rest I believe some would call…history. The couple dated for four years and then married each other a couple of months after graduation. Eventually, the Lord led them back to live and rear their new family in Montgomery. Of course, I'm referring to my own wonderful mother and father.

Mom's entire family's living in Minneapolis set up some very long road trips for my family. "Off to grandmother's house we go" took on a whole new meaning when taking into consideration the distance between Alabama and Minnesota! Here's the clincher: I hate road trips. I know; how terrible, right? Most people love the open road, and the thought of a nice, long trip is appealing to them. That's not me; in fact, I'm not one of those people by any stretch of the imagination. I've had friends over the years who have asked me about taking a road trip with them. To me, it doesn't matter if the road trip's a couple of hours or across the country; my answer is always the same—"No thanks."

It's not that I had some miserable, scarring childhood experience with car trips. I just don't like them in general. First of all, there are six people in my family, including three girls. Do you have any idea what that means? For one thing, it means luggage—lots of luggage. Nothing ruins a car trip like having your sister's suitcase (the one dedicated solely to hair-care products) sitting in your lap the whole way. Lots of luggage also means that we are each allotted about three square inches of leg room. For a kid with arthritis, three inches just doesn't cut it! Just to finish off with my feelings about luggage —why does my family always seem to get a third-floor motel room? I mean, really…whom did we offend in life to assure ourselves a permanent spot on the top floor of the motels that just happen not to have elevators? Pray for me, I'm having a difficult time getting over that one…

Secondly, road trips imply long periods of time where I can't do… well…anything. I've never been able to read in a moving car, so reading is obviously not an option. Listening to music is out of the question because Dad always listens to sermon tapes at a near-deafening decibel. (Ah, such good memories, Dad…love you!) I can sleep for a little while; but honestly, after the first couple of hours, I'm just too bored to drift off. Furthermore, I should point out the fact that drinking as much as you want is absolutely not allowed on our family road trips. And using the bathroom as often as you want is also strictly forbidden. Take that rule however you will.

If we were flying to Minnesota, let me tell you I'd be excited. I'd be looking forward to the trip more than I can tell you. But driving for two days straight? That's not exactly what I classify as a great time. So far my family has made two road trips from our house in Alabama to Minnesota. Each time I anticipated the trip with dread. Don't get me wrong. I was very much looking forward to seeing my extended family, and I was even excited about spending time with my immediate family. But the ride there and back? That was a different story altogether.

I didn't want to ruin the trip for anyone else, though. So I tried hard to keep my inhibitions about the road trip to myself. But with each impending trip, I always climbed into my crammed little cubicle of space that had been designated for me and my sister's suitcase with a sense of resignation. I wasn't looking forward to the trip. I wasn't excited about it. I wasn't embracing the journey. I was just tolerating it. I began the trip with a feeling of acceptance, and that was it.

An interesting phenomenon occurred on each trip, however. My sense of resignation always eventually melted away to make room for exhilaration and genuine enjoyment. My parents always seemed to pack enough memorable events into the road trip that I never really had time to think about how miserable I had planned on being. Lakeshore Drive in Chicago, Illinois, made me forget about my sister's suitcase. The Sears Tower and Mall of America were enough to make me forget about my utter lack of leg room. And going to a Minnesota Twins baseball game and the Museum of Science and Industry tipped me over the edge. I was actually...gasp...having fun! Somewhere along the way, I transformed from an attitude of mere acceptance to a joy-filled mind-set of embracing.

I believe that's the next step when it comes to the difficulties in our life as well. At this point, may I say that I hope that you have accepted all of the trials that God has given to you. But we can't stop there with merely accepting them. We have to take the next step; it's time to turn the corner. We'll never do anything for Christ if all we ever do is tolerate and accept the pain in life. It's good to accept it, but that's only the first step, and it's not the only step. The next step is just as important as the first. It's time to move past dealing with our difficulties...now it's time to fall in love with them. It's time to embrace.

Let me say from the onset that I fully intend to challenge the entire mind-set that most people have about trials and tribulations. By the end of this section of the book, I pray that you will be on your knees thanking God for whatever pain He has brought into your life. I know for many of you that will be a tough endeavor, but I believe it is absolutely critical. We must reach the point where we are happy that God has given us weaknesses. We have to joy in our individual hindrances. We must fall in love with God for caring enough about us to make us unique and special in His image. We must fall in love with God for wanting us to become all He has for us so much that He is willing to afflict us. We must fall in love with our "cup" because it makes us who we are and opens doors that would never be opened without it.

My desire is for you to become friends with your pain. I want you to thank God for it. I want you to be happy and upbeat. I want you to fall in love.

Almost always when we think about falling in love, we begin to picture in our mind some beautiful object. You think about your spouse if you have one. Maybe you think about your girlfriend or boyfriend with whom you are currently developing a relationship. Perhaps you envision your family and everything that they mean to you.

We also tend to picture material things. One of my friends just bought a Mustang convertible. Let me tell you…he's in love! But quite often we think about cars, boats, jewelry, and many other tangible items that captivate our attention. All of these items have a factor of commonality. We would classify them as blessings. We think of them as "good things." A spouse, a friend, a family, a car, and a lovely piece of jewelry would all be considered pleasant parts of life.

Probably most of us would never dream about considering our trials and difficulties as a blessing. My arthritis isn't beautiful, right? It's ugly. It's painful. It's not something that is attractive or pleasant. I shouldn't love it; it only seems that I should loathe it, right?

You surely wouldn't think of your pain as pretty, would you? The cancer that takes away a person's strength isn't cosmetically appealing. The emotional scars of depression and grief don't put a bright smile on your face. The burdens and cares of this world do not contribute to a beautiful exterior that can be embraced. That's more the way we tend to view pain, isn't it?

Think about how the world treats a "disabled" (I hate that label with a passion) person, for example. Throughout history, nearly any form of an ailment has been considered by humans as unfortunate, sad, and a disadvantage. Human nature sympathizes with those who are not healthy and whole. Special parking places, restrooms, and employment opportunities have been provided for these people because we feel sorry for them, and we certainly don't want to discriminate against those who already have such a burden to bear. That's the world's mind-set of difficulty.

Please don't misunderstand me. I'm not trying to say that any of these services shouldn't be happening. I am by no means trying to declare war on handicapped restrooms. But I truly believe that when viewed from a Biblical perspective, our pain and weakness is not something that should be viewed so negatively. In fact, it should be embraced, rejoiced over, and loved wholeheartedly as a gift from our loving Heavenly Father. That may be a foreign concept to many, but I believe it's the truth. And I don't just believe it's the truth because it's what the Bible teaches—though that's enough. I believe it's true because I have lived it. I have experienced it firsthand through the grace and power of Christ!

Sometimes you will hear someone say toward the end of his life that he wouldn't change a thing. I'm only a young man, yet I would change plenty about my life so far. But all of the changes I'd like to make would be to correct stupid decisions that I've made, like that time when I put Mr. Potato Head in the microwave to see if I could make mashed potatoes? Yeah, I'd really like to take that one back! But there is absolutely nothing about any of the difficulties which I have experienced that I have any desire to change or alter in the least. I mean that completely and sincerely. The truth is, I wouldn't want to live my life without the tumors, the arthritis, the uveitis, and the ramifications of those illnesses. God wants you to have the same opinion of the trial that He has given to you. God doesn't want us to hate the fire. He wants us to love it. Our Creator doesn't desire for us to loathe our existence and the difficulties that make up our lives. Rather He wants us to embrace them.

Let me emphasize at this point that you can do it. Right now you might be in the middle of the most tempestuous time of your life, and you really can't understand how in the world you could ever be happy about your trials. You might be so blinded by the storm clouds that you can't see the walls of the tunnel—much less light at the end. I know because I've been there, too. I'm writing this book not because I'm a theologian who can share a hundred verses on how to overcome your trials. I don't have a doctrinal degree or a Ph.D. in Bible. I am writing this book because I sincerely believe God has called me to do it, but also because I've cried out with a broken and scared heart to Christ all night long. I know the valleys that someone who is afflicted will experience. I also know the mountaintop experiences that God wants us to enjoy.

Chances are you know at least one happy person in life. You can count on at least one person whom you know to almost always have a smile on his face and a bounce in his step. I have no doubt that person has gone through a tough time, too. He has endured hardship and heartache. Remember, we've already addressed the fact that everyone has pain in his life. In fact, the happiest people that I personally know are those who I believe have experienced the most severe of difficulties and a searing level of pain.

One such person is a dear young lady whom I have been blessed enough to know for a little over a year now. As I have become friends with her, she has slowly revealed to me some of her background. I can't go into everything that she has endured in life, but let me say that in my estimation, she has been forced to go through more than anyone should ever have to endure in an entire lifetime—and she's only 19 years old. But there is a reason why I am such good friends with this girl. She's so happy—all the time. She keeps me laughing all the time. She's bright and energetic. Her impact on my life is a constant ray of sunshine. How does a lady who has endured inexplicable tragedy in her young life have such a genuinely and sincerely happy attitude in life? She has found the secret of not just tolerating the trials of life, but also embracing them.

What is that secret? What are the steps that we must take in order to truly fall in love with the pain that God has brought into our life? That's what I will address in this chapter. I hope and pray that we will soon realize that our difficulty is beautiful. I hope we will see that our pain should be cherished, our weakness should be loved, and our trouble should be embraced.

God Created You Uniquely

Psalm 139:1-14, "*O Lord, thou hast searched me, and known me. ²Thou knowest my downsitting and mine uprising, thou understandest my thought afar off. ³Thou compassest my path and my lying down, and art acquainted with all my ways. ⁴For there is not a word in my tongue, but, lo, O Lord, thou knowest it alto-*

*gether. ⁵Thou hast beset me behind and before, and laid thine hand upon me. ⁶Such knowledge is too wonderful for me; it is high, I cannot attain unto it. ⁷Whither shall I go from thy spirit? or whither shall I flee from thy presence? ⁸If I ascend up into heaven, thou art there: if I make my bed in hell, behold, thou art there. ⁹If I take the wings of the morning, and dwell in the uttermost parts of the sea; ¹⁰Even there shall thy hand lead me, and thy right hand shall hold me. ¹¹If I say, Surely the darkness shall cover me; even the night shall be light about me. ¹²Yea, the darkness hideth not from thee; but the night shineth as the day: the darkness and the light are both alike to thee. ¹³For thou hast possessed my reins: thou hast covered me in my mother's womb. ¹⁴I will praise thee; **for I am fearfully and wonderfully made**: marvellous are thy works; and that my soul knoweth right well."*

This passage of Psalm 139 is one of my favorite portions of the Bible. To me it so eloquently embodies the wonderful nature of Christ. It doesn't matter where we are, where we go, or what we do, we will never be able to remove ourselves from the awesome protection and guidance of our Lord. I love the verse when the Psalmist David observes that such knowledge is too wonderful for us!

We cannot possibly understand or comprehend the dominance and righteousness that is God Almighty! This section of Scripture is so beautiful though because it spends the first 13 verses building up and promoting the majesty and greatness of God. And then, in verse 14, David so wonderfully ties together how the awesome omnipresence of God directly impacts our lives. Psalm 139:14, *"I will praise thee; for I am fearfully and wonderfully made: marvellous are thy works; and that my soul knoweth right well."*

God doesn't make mistakes! We know that fact in our head, but do we believe that in our heart and soul? The "Sunday school" answer is pretty simple. Yes, we all recognize the fact that God is holy and perfect in nature. But sometimes I believe a touch of subconscious doubt seeps into our thinking when we are looking at the heartaches of life instead of the goodness of our Creator. We tend to focus so much on what is going wrong with our life that we quickly allow ourselves to think, "Wow! God blew that one!"

Maybe you have looked at your life and thought, "Whoa, what happened here?" The situations and circumstances just don't make sense to you. That's when the Christian must remind himself that his human thoughts are not God's thoughts and his human ways are not God's ways. God doesn't make mistakes! He doesn't mess up. He literally can't, remember? When we look at the difficulties in life, we have to continually remind ourselves that God ordained each and every one of those hardships. He also made us fearfully and wonderfully. Our difficulties and trials are a part of who we are. Put it all together and see that the pain and trouble in life is part of what makes us wonderfully and perfectly created by a Father Who cannot make a mistake.

It is so important for us to realize that God has created us specifically and individually. He made you special. He made me special. He made you unique. He made me unique. He made you perfectly. He made you exactly the way that you need to be. He molded you. He created you. He took His time. He thought about you. *"Before I formed thee in the belly I knew thee; and before thou camest forth out of the womb I sanctified thee, and I ordained thee a prophet unto the nations."* (Jeremiah 1:5)

Before my parents ever knew each other, God knew me. God designed my life perfectly before the beginning of time. God designed your life as well. Doesn't that thought comfort you? It does me. And furthermore, we are made in the image of God Himself. Genesis 1:26, 27 says, *"And God said, Let us make man in our image, after our likeness: and let them have dominion over the fish of the sea, and over the fowl of the air, and over the cattle, and over all the earth, and over every creeping thing that creepeth upon the earth. So God created man **in his own image**, in the image of God created he him; male and female created he them."*

That thought brings an indescribable blessing, but it also comes with a tremendous responsibility. What's the responsibility? Christ suffered dearly. And if we are made in the image of God, then we have to suffer as well. However, this suffering that we experience during our life is not supposed to make us sad or upset. *"But rejoice, inasmuch as ye are partakers of Christ's sufferings; that, when his glory shall be revealed, ye may be glad also with exceeding joy."* (I Peter 4:13) Christ was a sufferer; so we are as well. Thank God that we have been afforded the opportunity to be in the image of God and that He created us with a specific purpose—and with a specific trial or difficulty in mind!

Whatever it is, your weakness in life helps make you the wonderful person that God intended you to be. My medical problems are a part of who I am. They don't define me; they don't characterize me. But they are part of Dave McCroskey, and they always will be. That's who God wants me to be. And if a loving, tender Heavenly Father created me the way that I am, I'm going to embrace that knowledge. I'm unique. I'm special, and so are you!

God Has Given Us an Opportunity

Life is full of opportunities. Everywhere you look, there is an open door just waiting for exploration. Many years ago my grandfather offered me an opportunity to go with him to a NASCAR cup race in Daytona, Florida. Of course I was eager to go with my granddad, and I was very much looking forward to the trip (except for the car ride, of course!) Daytona International Speedway is one of the most popular racetracks in America, and I was so looking forward to seeing the best racecar drivers in the world competing against each other. Unfortunately, we found out when we reached Daytona that the race had been cancelled because of severe wildfires within a close proximity of the racetrack. We didn't turn the trip into a complete loss, of course. We ended up having a great time going to Sea World and doing some other sightseeing.

On the way home, my dad, who had come with us, started to laugh. I asked him what it was that had him laughing. He began to talk to his dad about a trip that they had taken many years earlier. When Dad was much younger, he and his family had taken a similar round-trip journey from Alabama to Florida. On the way back to Alabama, Dad had an idea. He decided that he wanted to stop the car right at the Alabama/Florida state line, get out of the car, and physically walk from one state into the other. He finally talked my granddad into letting him live out the idea, and my grandfather stopped the car so dad could walk from Florida to Alabama. That next week at school my dad enjoyed immensely being able to honestly tell all of his friends that he had walked all the way from Florida to Alabama by himself! My granddad asked me if I wanted to do the same thing. Of course I did! After all, like father, like son! So when we got right up to the point where we were going to cross into Alabama, my grandfather peeled off the road and stopped several feet short of the state line. I climbed out of the car and proudly walked all the way from Florida to Alabama!

That may seem like a fairly silly thing for me to do, but it was an unusual opportunity, to say the least, made available to me, and I took it. Can you say that you've done it? But I would have never gotten the chance to "walk from Florida to Alabama" if I would have never gotten in the car and begun the journey in the first place. Furthermore, I could have let the cancelation of the race ruin my attitude about the whole trip and decided not to enjoy myself for the rest of the time. A lousy attitude could have destroyed any desire within me to have any more fun.

The difficulties of our life also afford us opportunities and open doors. It is important to realize that our trials bring opportunities that we would never have without our pain and trouble. Maybe you are tempted to focus on everything that you've lost or can't do because of whatever your difficulty might be. Perhaps you are about to let an adverse attitude keep you from continuing to have fun and enjoy the happiness that God wants you to have. In Acts chapter five, Peter and several other apostles were put through some trials and temptations. Did they get discouraged? Did they get upset? No! Acts 5:41 reveals their response: *"And they departed from the presence of the council, rejoicing that they were counted worthy to suffer shame for his name."*

Christians are supposed to rejoice at the opportunities that they have been given by God through their trials. God can use Christians to glorify Him through their suffering. *"For I reckon that the sufferings of this present time are not worthy to be compared with the glory which shall be revealed in us."* (Romans 8:18) God wants us to completely forget about our suffering because we are so enraptured in the glory that He is revealing through us! But we will never be able to reach that point until we are willing to embrace the trials that God has given us.

Through the grace and power of God, we must continually force ourselves to embrace the opportunities that God is trying to present us through the trials of life. The story of Shadrach, Meshach, and Abednego is such a fantastically simple, yet powerful illustration of God's bringing His children through the fire. From that illustration, two key points must be examined.

God's Presence Makes All the Difference

"Then was Nebuchadnezzar full of fury, and the form of his visage was changed against Shadrach, Meshach, and Abednego: therefore he spake, and commanded that they should heat the furnace one seven times more than it was wont to be heated. [20]And he commanded the most mighty men that were in his army to bind Shadrach, Meshach, and Abednego, and to cast them into the burning fiery furnace. [21]Then these men were bound in their coats, their hosen, and their hats, and their other garments, and were cast into the midst of the burning fiery furnace. [22]Therefore because the king's commandment was urgent, and the furnace exceeding hot, the flame of the fire slew those men that took up Shadrach, Meshach, and Abednego." (Daniel 3:19-22)

The fire was so hot that the most mighty men in Nebuchadnezzar's army literally DIED just throwing the three Hebrew rulers into the fire. That's a hot fire! I've been around some pretty hot fires in my lifetime, but never anything that could possibly kill a man just by getting close to it. But I want to point out something very interesting in verses 23-26.

"And these three men, Shadrach, Meshach, and Abednego, fell down bound into the midst of the burning fiery furnace. [24]Then Nebuchadnezzar the king was astonied, and rose up in haste, and spake, and said unto his counsellers, Did not we cast three men bound into the midst of the fire? They answered and said unto the king, True, O king. [25]He answered and said, Lo, I see four men loose, walking in the midst of the fire, and they have no hurt; and

the form of the fourth is like the Son of God. [26] *Then Nebuchadnezzar came near to the mouth of the burning fiery furnace, and spake, and said, Shadrach, Meshach, and Abednego, ye servants of the most high God, come forth, and come hither. Then Shadrach, Meshach, and Abednego, came forth of the midst of the fire."* (Daniel 3:23-26)

Did you catch it? The mightiest men in the country were killed because of the intensity of the fire, but the king walked right up to the mouth of the furnace, and he was fine. Not only was Nebuchadnezzar unscorched, but the three men who were actually IN the fire were great, too. What made the difference? What suddenly made the burning, intense, and grueling fire so bearable for everyone? The presence of God made all the difference! It was the presence of the Almighty Saviour.

The presence of God is what will allow us to embrace our difficulty. He will make all the difference. We have to recognize and seek God's presence in our life. Without Him, we will be miserable, and we will be depressed. With Him we will be joy-filled, and we will be able to love the life that He has given to us.

How do we get the presence of God to help us endure the hardships and heartaches that come to us? *"Draw nigh to God, and he will draw nigh to you...."* (James 4:8) If we start seeking out God, we'll always find that He is right there. Where do we go to find Him? The same place He's always been! He's always been in our prayer-closets. He's always been in His Word. He's always been in His local New Testament church. We know where He is; the problem is that we do not always want to find Him. We become so upset and distracted by our pain that we lose the desire to grab hold of the One Who can make all the difference. It's no secret that we will have to get the presence and power of God back into our lives if we will ever have the strength not only to endure but to embrace our trials.

We Must Always Get Up

Get up? What does that phrase mean? The explanation is found in Daniel 3:23-25.

"And these three men, Shadrach, Meshach, and Abednego, fell

down bound into the midst of the burning fiery furnace. [24]*Then Nebuchadnezzar the king was astonied, and rose up in haste, and spake, and said unto his counsellers, Did not we cast three men bound into the midst of the fire? They answered and said unto the king, True, O king.* [25]*He answered and said, Lo, I see four men loose, walking in the midst of the fire, and they have no hurt; and the form of the fourth is like the Son of God."*

In verse 23 Shadrach, Meshach, and Abednego *"...fell down bound into the midst of the burning fiery furnace."* Notice what the king saw in verse 25. *"He answered and said, Lo, I see four men loose, walking in the midst of the fire...."* They were walking! At one point they had fallen down, but just a couple of verses later, the men were walking in the flames. Somewhere in between, they got up.

Have you gotten up yet? Fellow Christians, we will never be able to embrace and love our trial until we get up. With God's help, my friend, we have to get up—no matter what. You might be laid low right now. You might be knocked flat on your back at this moment. You might be suffering and in agony for the time being. But you must get up. *"For a just man falleth seven times, and riseth up again...."* (Proverbs 24:16) Promise God right now that no matter what happens, you will always get up. Promise yourself that you aren't going to stay down when life knocks you to your knees.

Sometimes we get so scared of getting back up because we grow afraid of what will happen to us when we do. The answer to that thinking is found in II Timothy 1:7: *"For God hath not given us the spirit of fear; but of power, and of love, and of a sound mind."* God hasn't given us that fear. That fear comes from our own sinful self. We must reject our own fear and insecurities, and we have to get back up; *"...and having done all, to stand. Stand therefore...."* (Ephesians 6:13, 14)

Too often it is so easy to fall into the trap which Job eventually fell into during all of the terrible tragedies that he endured. Job said, *"Man that is born of a woman is of few days, and full of trouble."* (Job 14:1) That's the way we feel many times, isn't it? Life is short, and life is hard. People can become so focused on their pain and trials that they completely miss out on the joy that God still wants for them. I Peter 1:6-8 reads,

> *"Wherein ye greatly rejoice, though now for a season, if need be, ye are in heaviness through manifold temptations: That the trial of your faith, being much more precious than of gold that perisheth, though it be tried with fire, might be found unto praise and honour and glory at the appearing of Jesus Christ: Whom having not seen, ye love; in whom, though now ye see him not, yet believing, ye rejoice with joy unspeakable and full of glory."*

Sometimes for a season it's okay to be sad due to the pain that we are experiencing, but God quickly wants us to get right back to *"joy unspeakable and fully of glory."*

Where are you today? Are you embracing every aspect of your life? Are you living a life of unspeakable joy? Are you thanking God for everything that He has given you—including the difficulties? Have you fallen in love with His plan for your life? Hebrews 12 contains the well-known parallel of our lives to a race that we must run. *"Wherefore seeing we also are compassed about with so great a cloud of witnesses, let us lay aside every weight, and the sin which doth so easily beset us, and let us run with patience the race that is set before us, Looking unto Jesus the author and finisher of our faith; who for the joy that was set before him endured the cross, despising the shame, and is set down at the right hand of the throne of God."* (Hebrews 12:1, 2)

Jesus was given a race to run. His race was to endure the Cross and the agony of dying for a lost, sinful world. He ran that race. But not only did He run the race, but He ran His race with joy. He was happy to submit to the will of God for His life, and He gladly shed His blood for the remission of sins. God has not called us to do anything to that magnitude, has He? No, of course not! Whatever He has given to us, however, we can do. We can run our race that He has designed with us uniquely in mind. We can run our race with patience. We can run the race with joy, happiness, and excitement. It's possible! I know it's possible to embrace your difficulties, weakness, and pain. It's possible, with God's help, to fall in love!

CHAPTER FIVE

BLESSINGS IN DISGUISE

The Blessings of Difficulty

D ifficulty is not a negative concept. I know it's a simple, yet novel concept to some. As I alluded to in another chapter, too many people have the mistaken idea that pain, trials, and difficulties are not beneficial and therefore certainly should not be embraced. The problem with this mind-set is not only that it severely limits our ability to take advantage of our pain, but that it also opens the door to our believing a lie. The idea that difficulty is bad for us is utterly false. Instead, it is a lack of resistance in life that is harmful to us.

Think about a well-trained athlete and his relationship with difficulty. Before a big event, he spends a significant amount of time in preparation. Maybe he trains for weeks, months, or even years. During this segment of training, the athlete puts his body through a vigorous regimen of exercise. Depending on the event of course, the athlete's workout program would almost assuredly contain quite a bit of resistance exercise. He would lift weights, push and pull against solid objects, and in general, try to maximize the strain on his body. If he is really working hard toward a goal, he is probably going to willingly put himself through a significant amount of pain during the process. He will be sore. He will hurt. He will probably end up doing damage to his body that will take time to heal. However, he does all of this preparation because he knows it's worth it. When all the pain, weights, and soreness disappear, he will a better athlete than he was before. He will be stronger, faster, and more capable of effectively and efficiently using his body. The resulting benefits far outweigh the difficulty.

It's the same way with our difficulty as well. It hurts and the resistance is hard, but in the end, our difficulty makes us a better Christian. It makes us spiritually fit. It transforms that weak and vulnerable flesh into a strong, resilient individual who can overcome and help others conquer their weaknesses as well. If we never had the testing, we would continue to be weak and completely unable to withstand even the small difficulties that God gives to us.

Consider the athlete and his training for a moment. Do you think the athlete hated his weights and exercise equipment? It's not a completely cut and dry answer. The answer to that question depends on what perspective the athlete decides to take. If you ask the athlete if he hates his weights and exercise equipment while he is toiling and straining at his gym, he very well might say yes. He is so focused on the pain and suffering that the resistance is causing him that his pain will probably have a negative opinion of his equipment. However, I imagine that almost all of the very well-trained athletes of the world would tell you that their equipment is very important to them. Ask a retired Olympian or a world-class athlete how he feels about his training regimen, and he will probably tell you that while it was sometimes hard, all of the hardships were worth it in the end. Those weights, machines, and equipment are all extremely precious to the best of athletes because athletes realize the blessings and benefits that their training will ultimately bring to them. All the sweat, the pain, and the adversity of the training is worth the strength and endurance that the athlete gains. In other words, the benefits far outweigh the difficulty.

Now if we substitute the difficulties that God has brought into our life for the weights in our sports analogy, there are quite a few similarities. Just like the weight equipment, your trouble and pain is hard to handle at times, but it also promises certain benefits to you as well. Too many Christians have such a counterproductive mind-set that their pain only brings negative consequences and by-products when the truth is that nothing could be further from the truth—or the Bible, for that matter. May I share a few examples of the positive benefits from our pain? It's time to stop dwelling on the negative and start focusing on the tangible as well as intangible blessings that God wants us to experience. Too often people are so consumed with what they perceive as the bad and painful that they lose all sight of the glorious and helpful.

The following is a short list of what I believe the Bible teaches are some of the numerous advantages to an afflicted person. However, mine is not an exhaustive list by any means. Some of these may not apply to you as specifically as they might apply to another person. Every trial is different, and therefore, every resulting benefit is distinctive as well. Do not let that stop you from giving this chapter a fair reading, however. I hope and pray that you will find many of these truths to be applicable to your situation and circumstance. For a few moments, forget about the pain, the suffering, and the affliction. Instead, for a few moments...focus on the benefits. Focus on the blessings. Only changing what we focus on will enable us to begin embracing the God-given difficulties of life.

Humility

I couldn't help but smile and shake my head as I began writing this chapter and thinking about all of the illustrations that I could write about how my chronic physical pain can crush my human pride. I remember as a 16-year-old becoming borderline obsessed with working out and exercising. I think that most teenage guys experience a stage where all they want to do is pump iron and flex muscles at some time or another. So it was with me. However, I didn't rush into this hobby without proper preparation and even research. I bought books and equipment, and I carefully outlined definite goals that I thought were achievable. Well, I'm afraid that while I was deciding on one particular goal, I temporarily forgot that I had a slightly disabling condition called rheumatoid arthritis! One of my goals was to be able to run one mile in less than eight minutes. Now, running an eight-minute mile would be a lofty goal for most people, but it is certainly achievable for a healthy person. I'm afraid that my body quickly reminded me that I am not what is commonly considered a healthy person. The fastest I ever ran was over 13 minutes! Talk about a blow to my well-developed male ego! I'm afraid it's very true: physical pain can certainly help cultivate a spirit of humility in a chronically pain-riddled Christian.

James 4:6 says, *"But he giveth more grace. Wherefore he saith, God resisteth the proud, but giveth grace unto the humble."* Two very distinct kinds of people are addressed in this verse. Furthermore, God seems to have two very distinct opinions on both of these groups of people. The first group would be those who are proud, and the Bible says that God resists this group of people. That, my friends, is abundantly clear, and I most definitely do not have any desire to belong to a group of people whom God Almighty literally resists.

However, another group of people of whom I would like to gladly call myself a member is mentioned in the verse. That group is the humble. Apparently God has a very different outlook on the humble as compared to the proud. The Bible says that God gives grace to the humble. I don't know about you, but as someone who has to deal with a good amount of pain in my life, I would love to have as much of the grace of God as I can get!

Obviously, pride can be a very destructive character trait in a person's life. The Bible says in Proverbs 16:18, *"Pride goeth before destruction, and an haughty spirit before a fall."* To me, this is one of the simplest verses in the Bible to interpret. Sometimes some very misguided people attempt to distort the interpretations of very clear verses in order to explain away a personal sin or to cause a division between the brethren. However, Proverbs 16:18 is not one of these verses. Allow me to put this verse into my own words: "If you have pride in your life, something very bad (destruction) will soon happen to you!" That's quite a clear interpretation.

Considering the promise of Proverbs 16:18, I think it's safe to assume that a Christian should make it a high-priority goal in his life to become as humble as possible. First of all, God is not a fan of pride and arrogance. I believe that has been established by both James 4:6 and Proverbs 16:18, and I could list several more verses proving this point if I thought it was necessary. Secondly, other people can't stand a proud person. All of us know someone who is arrogant, don't we? Do we have nice, fuzzy, admiring thoughts when we think about that person? Do we enjoy being with that person? Probably not!

Many times a difficulty or adverse situation is thought of as a blemish on a person's life, but I do not believe this is actually the case. However, it is very true that pride is a blemish on a person's life. Pride is a dangerous and despised sin; isn't it such a blessing to have a built-in mechanism that can help us with God's assistance to avoid such a transgression? I think it is! If you have an adversity in your life, God has given to you a tangible, built-in defense to help defeat the sin of pride. What a privilege, and what a blessing!

Determination/Strength

I realize that I am just slightly biased, but I honestly believe that the Lord has given to me the most Godly parents of all time. My parents have sacrificed immensely on my behalf throughout the last 18 years of my life. However, I believe what I am most grateful for is the fact that my parents have never treated me differently because of my medical problems. Many parents with a disabled child try to bubble wrap their child in order to avoid the risk of worsening the severity of his respective condition. Thank God my parents have never tried to do that! Besides the medications, doctor visits, and pain, I have been the closest thing to an average kid that one could be. I played basketball on a team for a total of four seasons. I play classical guitar. I have never opted out of any kind of a game (soccer, tackle football, etc.) because of my arthritis. I have mowed yards for hire since I was eleven years old. I've never done any less schoolwork than normal kids have because of my arthritis. There is nothing that I have not done because of my arthritis.

My parents have always told me that there is nothing that I cannot accomplish and that my arthritis is merely a part of me—not my defining characteristic. Because of this kind of parental support, I have developed a real sense of determination concerning the difficulties that I face due to my arthritis. I tell myself that as soon as I allow myself to give in or give up, I have allowed my arthritis to define me. If I allow my arthritis to define me, then that will be what people think of when they think of me. That's not what I want though. When people think of me, I want them to think about someone who is blessed by God and someone who wants to serve God with his life. Therefore, I fight, struggle, and pray so that I can glorify God with my life—not be the "poster boy" for disabled children who gave up.

I know of many kids who have done just that—given up. I go to an arthritis clinic every three months in Birmingham, Alabama, to see my rheumatologist. Usually 20 to 30 other children are there who have rheumatoid arthritis. Most of them limp, but they are certainly able to walk. However, usually three or four kids are there who cannot walk or who choose not to walk. These kids, or maybe their parents, have decided that they do not want to deal with the pain and the adversity anymore, so they just sit in their wheelchair and get wheeled around by their parents. They have no sense of determination. They could walk; they just don't. I don't look down on these kids because I know that it's hard, but I do feel sad on their behalf.

That's no way to live, my friend! I often wonder if these kids will just give up in every other area of their life too? If their job gets tough, will they quit and move on? If their marriage gets rough, will they just walk out? If a tragedy occurs, will they give up on God? This is a real concern, isn't it? In my mind, this is one of the major problems with my generation. There is no determination. I see this issue in my peers all the time. I see teenagers who have great potential, but they don't have the determination and character to reach that potential. They don't have enough determination to stay pure, so they end up complicating their lives in completely unnecessary ways. They don't have enough determination to build a strong relationship with God, so when tragedy strikes their life, they don't know how to handle it. They don't have enough determination to honor their parents like the Bible tells us to do, so they fill their life with stress and tension. Many problems would be solved if more people had more determination. Determine to do something, and then with God's help, do it!

Consider the average level of determination that people have with other people. If somebody is rude to us one time, that's it; we never try to talk to that person again. In fact, we often avoid that person from that point forward because that's the easy and simple thing for us to do. Did it ever cross our mind that just maybe that person needs a friend? Imagine if God had the same spirit of determination with us that we do with other people! What if God would have just ignored Adam and Eve after they directly disobeyed Him in the Garden of Eden? What if God had turned His back on you the first time you committed a sin against Him? I shudder when I think about where I would be if God became unconcerned about my life. We really should determine to be friendly with the other people who cross our path.

This really hits home with me right now because I have been trying to break through a wall of communication with a particular person whom I have known for nearly two years. This person has never been rude to me, but we've certainly never been close. Within the last month though, this person has slowly started to open up to me. It has been so wonderful for me to finally break through to this person. I could have just given up two years ago and resigned myself to never having a relationship with this person, but I am surely glad I didn't. I believe I owe any tenacity I possess to the sense of determination that I have cultivated in my life because of my pain.

What would my life look like in ten or twenty years without a spirit of determination? My guess is that it wouldn't be very pretty. I probably would have gone to college, but I wouldn't have graduated because somewhere along the way things would have gotten hard, and I would have given up because I wouldn't have any determination. I might have gotten married, but how long would that have lasted without any determination? I probably would've gone through many, many jobs because no job is perfect forever. Obviously, a sense and spirit of determination is extraordinarily important in our lives. It might be easy to overlook determination as a blessing that can stem from a disability or difficulty, but in my mind it definitely makes the list. The pain and the adversity force us to decide whether we will have a spirit of determination or if we will just give up. Hopefully, you have chosen to be a determined person. If you have chosen this route, there is a good chance you owe it solely to two things: your physical pain and the grace of God. Praise the Lord!

Faith

Let me with all humility admit at the beginning of this chapter that, as an 18-year-old, I make no pretense that I thoroughly grasp all of the theological nuances of faith. In fact, faith is an area that I feel completely unqualified to address with any authority whatsoever. I believe that I feel this way because I don't possess as much faith as what I'd like to have in my own life. That being stated, however, it would be unthinkable to leave out faith while writing about the blessings that come from the trials and tribulations of life. Therefore, with God's help, I will try to concisely make a case for faith's being a benefit of difficulty.

I have heard faith described and defined in many different ways, but usually these definitions are too complicated for me to adequately comprehend. To me, faith is simply reliance. For example, when I sit in a chair, I am relying on that piece of furniture to hold my body weight. I have faith in that chair's ability. In the same way, I have faith in God's ability. I have that reliance because He is my Creator and Saviour. Nobody has ever or could ever do for me what Christ has already done. That is why I put my faith in God.

So that definition brings us to the question of how faith is a benefit that stems from adversity in a Christian's life. Let me begin by irrevocably stating that having a great amount of faith in Christ is grand! I know that seems so obvious that it barely warrants mentioning, but it is true, and sometimes simple truth can make the most profound difference. Therefore, since the more faith the better, every Christian should make it one of his goals to grow and nurture as much faith as possible. This is where our pain comes into the picture. The more things that we cannot do because of our problems, the more things we can allow God to do for us! Naturally, people do not want to rely on anyone else any more than they have to. People generally want to do things for themselves, and more importantly, people want to do things their way. However, sometimes people like me with a physical challenge cannot do everything for themselves. I know personally that there are many things that I simply cannot do. I could not even begin to enumerate the number of tasks that I cannot do because of my physical limitations.

I immediately think of one major area when I consider how a Christian should use his pain to help grow his faith. Christians should have faith in Christ to provide for the extra earthly needs that result from having a specific difficulty. I use the word "extra" because every Christian should rely on God to take care of his needs. However, I am stressing the fact that with extra and specific needs come extra and specific ways for God to grow a person's faith.

The key here is to pinpoint the areas that cause us difficulty and use them to grow our faith. A difficulty can be anything. It could be a large burden such as the medical debt that my family faced, or it can be something much smaller. One of the biggest annoyances that I have with my arthritis is that my joints are very stiff in the mornings. I am sure that many people can relate to this feeling. Now morning stiffness is not huge, but there have been many nights when I have simply told God, "I don't want to be stiff in the morning. Please help me to move around in my bed enough while I sleep so that I won't be so stiff when I wake up."

I didn't ask for a miraculous healing. I simply asked the Lord to help my body to move around naturally while I slept. Let me testify, there are very few mornings that I wake up stiff after I have prayed that prayer! Again, this is my point. Someone who does not struggle with a difficulty (i.e. morning stiffness) never has the opportunity to see God answer his prayers in the same exact way. That is why I argue that our difficulties are really blessings when viewed from the correct perspective. Instead of complaining about a silly thing like morning stiffness, I am able to get a firsthand glimpse of God's flexing His muscle in my life, thereby growing my faith in Him. So whatever your "extra" or "special" need is, whether it's chemotherapy, blindness, medical debt, or some seemingly little, tiny thing like morning stiffness, allow God to provide for your needs while you sit back and watch the power of God in action!

Patience

I hate to admit it, but I've never been a terribly patient person. I like to know what's happening, when it's happening, and most of the time I'd just as soon like to know why it's happening, too. That's not too much to ask, is it? I manage to survive most of the time without becoming overly anxious about the events of life with one glaring exception: Christmas presents. Whoever thought up the idea of Christmas presents really hated kids, you know? Knowing that there are presents to be had…but you can't have them until the twenty-fifth of December…that's cruel and unusual in my book.

My parents never even tried to play up the whole Santa Claus ruse in our minds. They told us all along that Mom and Dad bought the gifts and wrapped everything themselves. Never believing in Santa Claus was fine with me, but what wasn't fine with me was that not keeping up appearances for Santa meant that my parents saw no need to keep the presents hidden until the night before Christmas. As my mom would buy the gifts, she would wrap them and place them under our Christmas tree. That's like torture. Seriously, having to sit and look at presents for weeks before you can open them—people have justifiably gone to jail for putting their children through far less than that.

But here was the part that made things unbearable to me. My parents would brag about how when they were kids, they would always carefully unwrap all of the presents before Christmas so that they could see what they were going to get. Then they would covertly rewrap the gifts and place them back under the tree, hoping their parents would not notice. My mom seemed to fondly recall her own Grandpa's helping her unwrap and rewrap her presents every year.

At that point, not only was I dying of impatience, but I was actually beginning to feel as if I were missing out on a vital part of everyone's childhood. From listening to my parents, it sounded like the whole reason parents wrapped gifts in the first place was so their kids could secretly open them and then put everything back before they got caught. Obviously, I was supposed to do this, too. I wouldn't be a good kid if I didn't, right?

So one year I finally worked up the nerve to give it a shot. I judiciously picked the gift that I was going to unwrap, took it to my bedroom when my mom wasn't looking, and then unwrapped a really nice athletic shirt. I truly liked the gift, but then it was time to put things back where they went before anyone got a drift of what was happening.

Here is where I ran into a little bit of trouble. I had never wrapped something in my life! My sister, Angela, always used to wrap presents for me because sometimes it was hard because of my arthritic hands. Now I was stuck. I quickly found out I wasn't going to be able to successfully and neatly wrap the shirt, but neither could I tell Angela what I had done. Now I was panicking! In fact, I was really worried at this point. What if Mom and Dad found out and were really upset? Maybe they wouldn't let me have the shirt. Maybe they wouldn't let me have any of my presents. Maybe they'd banish Christmas forever. This was a dilemma of incomparable proportion for a ten-year-old. My only option was to do the best I could with re-wrapping the present. My best…well, wasn't good. A couple of days later my mom discovered a partially unwrapped gift with my name on it. It didn't take too much guessing for her to figure out what had happened. My parents exercised quite a bit of mercy in this situation, and they didn't punish me with anything but a stern lecture on the necessity of patience.

My lack of patience could have dearly cost my ten-year-old, Christmas-present-starved self. Instead of just enduring the temptation of the appealing looking presents stacked under our family Christmas tree, I gave in impatiently. However, insufficient patience can have an impact on our life that is far more negative than having one's parents take away a Christmas present. Impatience is a problem that can rob a child of God of some of the most valuable items in his life. It can ruin the perfect timing of God's will, costing the Christian invaluable relationships or at the least the eternal satisfaction of waiting until the time is right. The Bible teaches that there is a time for everything, but getting everything to line up with the will of God is the tricky part sometimes.

"To every thing there is a season, and a time to every purpose under the heaven: ²A time to be born, and a time to die; a time to plant, and a time to pluck up that which is planted; ³A time to kill, and a time to heal; a time to break down, and a time to build up; ⁴A time to weep, and a time to laugh; a time to mourn, and a time to dance; ⁵A time to cast away stones, and a time to gather stones together; a time to embrace, and a time to refrain from embracing; ⁶A time to get, and a time to lose; a time to keep, and a time to cast away; ⁷A time to rend, and a time to sew; a time to keep silence, and a time to speak; ⁸A time to love, and a time to hate; a time of war, and a time of peace." (Ecclesiastes 3:1-8)

What a beautiful portion of Scripture illustrating the fact that there is a time and a place for everything—including opening Christmas presents! But when a lack of patience preempts the plans and times of God, it can lead to very serious consequences. By this time, you should be picking up on what's coming next. What could possibly help us cultivate patience in our life? I'll give you three guesses, and the first two don't count. That's right! It's our difficulties and trials! James 1:2-4 teaches,

"My brethren, count it all joy when ye fall into divers temptations; ³*Knowing this, that the trying of your faith worketh patience.* ⁴*But let patience have her perfect work, that ye may be perfect and entire, wanting nothing."*

The trials that God brings us through will result in a more patient and content spirit. Furthermore, when we allow patience to truly take hold as a continually present attitude in our life, we can literally reach the point where we are what the Bible calls *"entire."* In other words, the pain and trouble of our life is a blessing because it allows us potentially to reach a state of *"wanting nothing."* What a calm and peaceful place!

Relationship With God

Whether or not you have a walk with God is quite possibly the most important aspect of a person's day-to-day life. Perhaps it's naïve of me, but I think that nearly all Christians would say that they honestly desire a close relationship with God. However, many times life distracts us from the most important things. Sadly enough, seemingly few Christians can honestly claim to have a close walk with their Saviour. Too often we turn our backs on God and forget about His eternal goodness. What can God use to lovingly draw us back to Himself? The difficulties of life, of course! We see an example of God's methodology in II Chronicles 33.

"And the LORD *spake to Manasseh, and to his people: but they would not hearken.* ¹¹*Wherefore the* LORD *brought upon them the captains of the host of the king of Assyria, which took Manasseh among the thorns, and bound him with fetters, and carried him to Babylon.* ¹²*And when he was in affliction, he besought the* LORD

his God, and humbled himself greatly before the God of his fathers,
[13]And prayed unto him: and he was intreated of him, and heard
his supplication, and brought him again to Jerusalem into his
kingdom. Then Manasseh knew that the LORD he was God."

(II Chronicles 33:10-13)

The Word of God records that only when Manasseh found himself in affliction did he seek the Lord. It's a shame that God often has to use affliction to bring His children back to Him, but it is obviously an effective tool. Also, let me point out that it is in our best interest. I know it hurts at times, but in the long run, being drawn to God is obviously in our best interest. Trials reveal to us just how desperately we need God's help and sustaining power. It all comes back to dependency. It is so critical that we realize the necessity of God. We can't do anything for ourselves. Without a deep, personal relationship with God, it is impossible to live a fulfilled and happy life.

It's so wonderful that God loves us so much that He is willing to allow us to suffer in order to help us see our need of Him. Thankfully, we don't have a Saviour Who is content with allowing us to wander misguided and ignorant through life. It is natural for us to drift from Christ. It's that "old man" who is continually trying to grab a foothold inside of us. In His great mercy, God has provided for struggles in our life to encourage us to die to ourselves and drive us to the only true God. As the Psalmist put it, *"Before I was afflicted I went astray: but now have I kept thy word."* (Psalm 119:67) David went astray from the Word of God until he was afflicted. Thank God for that affliction!

Hope

"And not only so, but we glory in tribulations also: knowing
that tribulation worketh patience; [4]And patience, experience; and
experience, hope; [5]And hope maketh not ashamed; because the
love of God is shed abroad in our hearts by the Holy Ghost which
is given unto us." (Romans 5:3-5)

This Scripture shows us that hope is another of the tremendous by-products of tribulation. According to I Corinthians 13, hope is one of the greatest virtues found in the Bible. *"And now abideth faith, hope, charity, these three; but the greatest of these is charity."* (I Corinthians 13:13)

Hope is sorely lacking in the world today. As I walk down the aisles of stores and glance into the eyes of my fellowman...I see a world full of people without hope. I see people who are wandering and searching for something that they don't believe they will ever find. Of course, we know from the Bible that we are to hope in God. *"And now, LORD, what wait I for? my hope is in thee."* (Psalm 39:7) But without Christ's in-dwelling a person, not much opportunity exists for hope. For a Christian, however, there is so much to hope for. We can hope in God's favor, His lovingkindness, and His mercy. We can hope for a life filled with eternal significance. We can earnestly hope for the eternity that we will spend in Heaven with our Creator and Saviour. Hope is a tremendous virtue that is also gained through difficulty. Thank God for hope for it *"...maketh not ashamed."*

Eternal Perspective

It really is a wonderful life! The blessings and privileges of life are wonderful and numerous. But nobody said that things were always going to be easy on earth. Without any exceptions whatsoever, everyone must go through the rigors and difficulties of life. At times, our circumstances seem so overwhelming that we are tempted to wonder if we will make it. Paul found himself in this position on one of his trips to Asia. *"For we would not, brethren, have you ignorant of our trouble which came to us in Asia, that we were pressed out of measure, above strength, insomuch that we despaired even of life."* (II Corinthians 1:8)

Paul literally reached a point where he didn't think he was going to survive. Have you been there? Does it feel like the crush of adversity is too much for you to handle? If you are there right now, that's not such a bad thing. It's good for us to realize that we can't make it or survive on our own. Thankfully, however, it's not up to us to deliver ourselves. We have Someone much more powerful than we are Who will help us in our time of need.

"But we had the sentence of death in ourselves, that we should not

trust in ourselves, but in God which raiseth the dead." (II Corinthians 1:9) Paul reminds us of a tremendous truth in this verse. It's not ourselves that we should trust to guide us through the trials of life. Rather, we are to rest in the power of a God Who raised Himself from the dead. That's a powerful God! If He is so mighty that He can raise Himself from the dead, He can handle whatever trouble we find ourselves in as well. It doesn't matter what we endure or what we have to deal with in life. He wants to help us through all of it. II Timothy 3:11 says, *"Persecutions, afflictions, which came unto me at Antioch, at Iconium, at Lystra; what persecutions I endured: but out of them all the Lord delivered me."* Psalm 34:19 says, *"Many are the afflictions of the righteous: but the LORD delivereth him out of them all."*

This brings me to the final advantage of pain and difficulty that I want to address in this chapter. Our adversity in life is a blessing to us because it helps us gain an eternal perspective. What do I mean by eternal perspective? Simply put: our pain allows us see where our help stems from. *"I will lift up mine eyes unto the hills, from whence cometh my help. My help cometh from the LORD, which made heaven and earth."* (Psalm 121:1-2) Every time we find ourselves in a difficult or troublesome situation in life, we should be reminded *"...from whence cometh my help."*

Think about how it would change our lives if we lived with the constant awareness of the power of Christ. Our pain helps us to do just that. We waste so much time and energy trying to sort out life on our own when we have a God Who wants to deliver us out of ALL tribulation. We have a loving Father Who has delivered us in the past, Who currently continues to deliver us, and Who wants to provide for us in the future as well. *"Who delivered us from so great a death, and doth deliver; in whom we trust that he will yet deliver us."* (II Corinthians 1:10)

Are you feeling even slightly better about your difficulties and trials? I hope so. Humility, determination, faith, patience, a relationship with God, hope, and an eternal perspective on deliverance are just some of the magnificent advantages that He wants us to experience because of our adversity. God has given us these challenges in life because He knows that they are in our best interest. Why then is it many times so difficult for us to see that? We must shift our focus. We must stop staring at the problems and look instead at the blessings. The truth is…the benefits outweigh the difficulties. Your cup is a blessing in disguise.

CHAPTER SIX

Such Things as Ye Have

Cultivating a Life of Contentment

I remember the night that I am about to describe so vividly that I can still feel the time dragging by, the blood dripping from my head, and the thread being pulled through my skin. I'm getting ahead of myself, though. When I was four years old, I was playing in my parents' bedroom with my five-year-old sister Angela. We were doing what all small children do when their parents aren't around—nothing good. What was our naughty activity of choice on this particular evening? We were having a gymnastics tournament on my parents' bed. Now Angela actually did gymnastics at a local armory, so she was able to perform cartwheels, handstands, and flips on the bed without endangering her life. I, however, had absolutely no prior experience in executing these same moves. This fact was proven when I went careening headfirst into the headboard of the bed. Thus began one of the most memorable nights in my young life.

At first I didn't feel any pain at all because I was so shocked that I had just bounced my head off of a wood surface. When I saw the blood though, I realized that this was probably not a good thing. This was the first time that any of the kids in my family had decided to put a gash in their head, so my mom was somewhat unsure of what to do. After a quick call to my pediatrician though, it was determined that a trip to the emergency room was in order. We rushed to the emergency room, and that was when the wait began.

Anyone who has gone to the local emergency room knows how these things work. If you have stomach pains resulting from eating an expired piece of sandwich meat, you are rushed to the doctor. If you are a grown man with a twisted ankle, you are moved to the top of the list. A small child bleeding from the back of his head takes no precedence whatsoever!

They seem to wait forever. So I sat with my mom holding a towel to my head for three hours before my name was finally called.

Almost immediately, a nurse came in to give me anesthesia. She then informed me that the doctor would be in to sew up my head in a minute. Her idea of a minute and my idea of a minute were vastly different! Four hours later the doctor came into my room. He nonchalantly explained to my mom that a lady had come in who was experiencing chest pains (probably a bad fish stick or something), so the doctor had to delay my treatment while he treated this lady. The doctor laid me face down on the table and began to stitch up my head. As he worked though, I began to cry. Why was I crying? I was in PAIN!

Well, my mom, who is gifted with a natural knowledge of when her children should be crying and when they should not, sensed that something was not right. My mom asked the doctor why I was crying when I had been given anesthesia. That was when it hit him. Suddenly, that doctor began envisioning himself living in a cardboard box and driving a grocery cart for the rest of his life! The doctor sorrowfully explained to me and my mom that the anesthesia had no doubt worn off sometime during the last four hours. This was lawsuit material, my friend! We didn't call any lawyers, though. We just tried to get out of the hospital as soon as possible.

On the way out of the hospital, we passed a vending machine. My mom asked me if I would like to have a bag of M&Ms. I was a four-year-old kid. What kind of question was that? That's like asking a blind man if he'd like to see! Yes! I wanted my very own bag of M&Ms! All of a sudden the bleeding head, the endless waiting, and the excruciating pain was pathetic in comparison to the sheer joy of having my own bag of M&Ms. At one o'clock in the morning, with my head sown up, walking out of the emergency room, I was happy and content.

Contentment is the next critical step that must be taken in order to embrace the difficulties in our life. Contentment is a virtue with which many people, even Christians, struggle, and it can be incredibly hard at times for someone who is very burdened in life to be content with the situations in which he finds himself. Just from a purely psychological standpoint, it is difficult to be content and satisfied when it seems like everything is going against us.

Think about someone you know in your life who isn't content with his circumstances—ever. I am recalling a dear family right now. These great people, who are fantastic Christians and very close friends of mine, are constantly making new plans and changing their goals in life. It seems like every other month or so, they are talking about packing up everything and moving somewhere new to explore a different opportunity that has been presented. They are basically, for all intents and purposes—completely unstable. Many people are never satisfied with their material possessions. Some people always need a new house, a new car, a new toy, etc. These people usually end up filing for chapter 11 more than once in the course of their life.

So many people seem to struggle with the simplistic concept of contentment. And I think that is one of the basic problems with the whole idea of contentment. It shouldn't be so difficult, but it is. Human nature is very ambitious (which isn't a terrible attribute in and of itself), but that ambition can result in a lack of contentment that can really complicate and cripple the life God would have us to lead.

A few key principles must be recognized and applied in our lives in order to cultivate a spirit of contentment and satisfaction about our lives and, of course, specifically concerning the limitations, weaknesses, and obstacles that we face.

Changing Your Mind-set

A big part of being "okay" with the heartaches that we must all experience in life is simply allowing God to change our mind-set. We have to let Him teach us how to be satisfied in every situation. Paul had to go through this transformation process, but he was a far happier person after God taught him contentment. *"Not that I speak in respect of want: for I have learned, in whatsoever state I am, therewith to be content. I know both how to be abased, and I know how to abound: every where and in all things I am instructed both to be full and to be hungry, both to abound and to suffer need."* (Philippians 4:11, 12) Can you claim to be content in whatever state you find yourself? Are you okay when the storms of life rage around you? Do you trust in God's grace and strength, or do you panic? It's so critical that we let God change our mind-set concerning the trials we endure.

Part of changing our mind-set involves realizing our own inability. What can we do to change our circumstances? Perhaps there are times when there are tangible steps that we can take to help our situation, but sometimes that is not the case. I can't change my arthritis. I can take medication, see doctors, and take care of my body, but at the end of the day, I can't magically wish the disease out of me. I can't change my eye problems.

Right now as I write this chapter, my right eye has taken a severe turn for the worse. A few months ago the retina in my right eye detached from the back eye-wall. I underwent a surgery quickly to repair the eye only to have the retina detach again two weeks later. The retina was surgically repaired again. This time it lasted about ten days. To the best of my doctor's knowledge, apparently there is serious damage to a component of my eye that is supposed to help naturally heal the eye. My doctors have told me in no uncertain terms that there is not much they can do. Either my eye will heal itself (that's doctor language for what we Christians know as God's performing a miracle), or I very well may not have sight in my right eye any longer.

As I write this book, I am endeavoring to be as transparent as possible in order to hopefully be as helpful as I can be. So here is a bit more honesty: I'm scared. I don't want to go blind in one of my eyes. I'd be lying if I said that I was resting perfectly in the knowledge of God's perfect plan for my life. I'm trying to keep my focus on God, but I am concerned about the health of my eye. As one unsuccessful surgery follows another, I am becoming increasingly aware of the possibility that I could have viewed something out of my right eye for the last time. I may never read with that eye again. I may never have peripheral vision on that side of my body again. These thoughts scare me. But at the same time, I feel the Holy Spirit of God asking me this question: "Who is in control?"

I really can't do anything about my eye situation right now. I can pray—and I am. I can take all of my medication the way I'm directed, and I do. I can show up to all of my appointments so that my doctors can monitor my eye properly, and my mom makes sure that happens. But at the end of the day...can I heal my eye? Can I make it all better? Can I restore my own sight? Of course not! I don't have that power or ability. There is nothing I can do in and of myself to "fix" things. The doctors can't do anything either. Trust me...they've tried. I've been on eye drops every hour for months now. I have had surgery after surgery. I have even had steroid injections administered straight into my eyeball. Yes, while I was awake. Believe me, when you lie on a table and watch as a needle descends right into your eye, you feel like you have tried everything there is. I've told people about these injections, and they say, "Yeah, well, it's not like it hurts, right?"

I wish! Let me tell you—it hurts. It's definitely one of the most painful procedures I've ever endured. And it's not just physically uncomfortable...it's physiological torture. This treatment would not get past the Geneva Convention! Having to lie completely still on a table while your eyelids are pulled back by a device that resembles barbecue tongs is pretty uncomfortable. But then the intense pressure of having a needle actually sticking out of your eye while the doctor pumps medication into your system is practically unbearable. Then of course you deal with the "foreign-object-in-my-eye" sensation for the rest of the day. Oh yeah...it's good times. But hey, it makes for a great story! All that to say, we've done everything...and everything has failed. The question becomes this: if I can't do anything...why should I be so scared?

Whether or not I go blind is completely in God's very capable hands. I'm content with that knowledge. If God chooses to heal me and restore my vision, I'm content with that decision. If God decides that I would be a more usable vessel without my right eye, I'm content with that choice as well. I really am. So why should I be worried? Why shouldn't I be content with the situation? If I'm not in control and I trust God to perform His will in the situation, then I should be satisfied with whatever happens. It's easier said than done, isn't it? But I'm praying that God will change my mind-set and replace my fear with a calming sense of peace.

Many years ago I wrote a short poem that embodies what I am trying to convey to you now. Guess what I entitled it even back then?

Contentment

I was amazed last Friday night
When I looked up in the sky
For one beautiful star
Caught my gazing eye.

Now you might say
One star would be a bore,
But let me ask a question—
Could you make any more?

I remember vividly the night to which I allude in this poem. I was at a friend's house late one night. His house was out in the country away from the city lights that I was accustomed to since I live right in the middle of an urban area. I was anticipating going outside after it got dark because I wanted to see a starry sky for once. For whatever reason, however, that night I searched and searched but could only see one star in the night's sky. I was very disappointed. Why wasn't there a beautiful display of glowing lights decorating the tranquil backdrop of a country night sky? But then the thought occurred to me in an instant…what could I do about it? I could stand outside all night long and not change how many stars were visible to my eyes. This was completely out of my control and realm of influence. So not only was my attitude wrong, but I was also missing out on enjoying the one magnificent star that God had hung in the sky for me to see (and learn from) that evening.

What a waste it is to focus on the stars that can't be seen instead of reveling in the one that is visible! Yet that is precisely how so many people live their lives and hence why they are never content with their circumstances. I haven't been able to see out of my right eye for three months at this point. You know what I'm figuring out? Life goes on. I can still do practically everything that I could do before. I can still drive.

I can read. There is nothing that I can think of that I can't do because of my blindness. It's a much better use of my emotions to focus on everything that I can still do and accomplish instead of being so preoccupied with the thought of never having vision in that eye again. Are there things or people that have been permanently taken from you? Perhaps you've had to say goodbye to someone or something forever. But aren't there still so many things left? Aren't there still opportunities and blessings that abound? Of course there are! With God's help, let's focus on those; *"...and prove me now herewith, saith the LORD of hosts, if I will not open you the windows of heaven, and pour you out a blessing, that there shall not be room enough to receive it."* (Malachi 3:10)

Recognize God's Presence

"Let your conversation be without covetousness; and be content with such things as ye have: for he hath said, I will never leave thee, nor forsake thee." (Hebrews 13:5) Contentment is a concept that I am continually reiterating throughout this book. Why? Because it's so important. It is absolutely critical to one's goal of accepting, embracing, and using the God-given difficulties of life. This verse from Hebrews eloquently enforces one of the ways that we can develop contentment with our circumstances and pain. Quite simply, we must recognize the presence of God in our lives. The Bible commands us to *"...be content with such things as you have"* and then tells us how we can accomplish this goal: *"for he hath said, I will never leave thee, nor forsake thee."* It's that constant reminder that He is never going anywhere that will give us the contentment that we all so desperately need in our life.

In Acts 27 the Scripture records Paul's being caught in a tremendous storm and eventually shipwrecked. The men on the ship were beginning to become quite fearful for their lives until Paul stood up to address them.

"And now I exhort you to be of good cheer: for there shall be no loss of any man's life among you, but of the ship. [23]*For there stood by me this night the angel of God, whose I am, and whom I serve.* [24]*Saying, Fear not, Paul; thou must be brought before Caesar: and, lo, God hath given thee all them that sail with thee.* [25]*Wherefore,*

sirs, be of good cheer: for I believe God, that it shall be even as it was told me." (Acts 27:22-25)

Paul had such a confidence, and dare I say contentment, about the storm because he was aware of the presence of God. I love it when Paul says, *"...be of good cheer... for I believe God...."* Doesn't that statement wondrously sum up what a person's attitude in life should be? It would be so much easier to be content and satisfied if a Christian just took the attitude of, "It doesn't matter what happens...I trust God." That's the end of it. It's that simple. We don't have to worry or fret. We can just believe Him and rest in the awareness of His presence.

We tend to get so panicked and restless when we are confronted with trials in life. That's our natural reaction, but it shouldn't be an acceptable way to behave ourselves. The Bible teaches that we should be firm and steadfast in a resolute embrace of the limitations that God has given us. *"That no man should be moved by these afflictions: for yourselves know that we are appointed thereunto."* (I Thessalonians 3:3) What a marvelous verse! We aren't supposed to be moved by afflictions! We shouldn't panic and "lose it." We should be like Paul...believing and resting in the wonderful presence of the God Who will never leave us nor forsake us. *"Be still, and know that I am God...."* (Psalm 46:10)

Recognize God's Provision

There is yet another step past realizing God's presence, however. His presence alone is magnificent, but what will truly allow us to develop a contented mind-set in life is to recognize that His presence translates into His awesome provision as well. I believe the provision that Christ offers His children is such a remarkable blessing that is sadly overlooked and taken for granted by Christians. *"But my God shall supply all your need according to his riches in glory by Christ Jesus."* (Philippians 4:19) Do we realize that this verse is a promise from God? A promise that He is absolutely supernaturally bound to keep? It is! He has assured each and every one of us that He will supply ALL of our needs with His immeasurable power.

I think the problem that we run into is that we have a different definition of "need" than God does. There is a verse in I Timothy that I believe provides us with a glimpse into what we should truly consider a "need" in our life.

> *"But godliness with contentment is great gain. ⁷For we brought nothing into this world, and it is certain we can carry nothing out. ⁸And having food and raiment let us be therewith content."*

(I Timothy 6:6-8)

The beginning of the verse points out the entire reason why I am writing this chapter. When we are able to combine and embody a Godly life with a contented spirit, we have greatly gained. We have opened new doors of opportunity to ourselves. We have finally succeeded in doing what God has called us to accomplish through our difficulties. We should make that a goal for the rest of our life. Through Christ's help, why don't we desperately try to lead a life full of Godly works intertwined with a satisfied and contented outlook.

Then the second part of the verse goes on to emphasize what is the central theme of what I'm trying to convey through this chapter. *"For we brought nothing into this world, and it is certain we can carry nothing out."* That thought really changes the perspective on what we define as a "need." When we were born, we had absolutely nothing. When we die, we are going to be able to keep absolutely no material possessions. So why do we end up getting so greedy in between the cradle and the grave? It seems like far too many people get a little bit older in their life, and all of a sudden the term "need" takes on an entirely new meaning. Suddenly cars, houses, vacations, retirement funds, technology, electronic gadgets, and a life full of ease and relaxation become "needs." What is truly a need? What do we Biblically have to have? *"And having food and raiment let us be therewith content."* If there are clothes on our body and food on our table, God has provided for us abundantly above that which we deserve.

The truth is though, that God has provided for us more than we could ever comprehend. Even those who are in the most dire of circumstances would not honestly be able to count the many blessings that they have received from their Heavenly Father. What child of God can truthfully claim that God has never provided for their necessities?

I don't believe that anyone could make such an accusation with a clear conscience. Mature Christians revel in the provision of God because they realize that what we have compared to what we deserve is nothing sort of breathtaking.

A healthy recognition of the awesome provision of God is certainly crucial to creating and retaining a contented spirit concerning the trials and difficulties of life. It would become so much easier to embrace the hardships and heartaches if we were continually and constantly aware of the fact that God will always provide for our needs. It doesn't matter what happens or which situations we find ourselves entrapped by. It shouldn't concern us what befalls us on a daily basis because we can rest upon the assurance that there is an Almighty God Who is constantly aware of our circumstance and enduringly ready to provide for our each and every need. What do you lack? Can you honestly look Heavenward and accuse God of failing to provide any need in your life? The truth of God's provision is embodied by the prophet Joel when he said, *"And ye shall eat in plenty, and be satisfied, and praise the name of the LORD your God, that hath dealt wondrously with you: and my people shall never be ashamed."* (Joel 2:26) We do eat and live in plenty. We should be satisfied. We should praise the name of our Lord because He has indeed dealt wondrously with us. And we certainly should never be ashamed. It is so much easier to be content with our difficulties and the pain in our life when we are constantly living in recognition of the fact that God will always provide for us.

Develop a Lowly Heart and Mind

You've met them. You have made the acquaintance of that person who is, in his mind, God's gift to mankind. These people are pretty much unstoppable, amazing, and utterly indispensable in every way. They take cocky and arrogant to a whole new, previously undiscovered level. Due to their indescribable brilliance, the world basically owes them. In exchange for their breathing the same air that we do, it is the entire world's responsibility to ensure their constant satisfaction and happiness. They deserve the promotion at work because…well…they just do. No, of course they don't actually work harder than anyone else, and they aren't particularly more productive or brilliant than other people, but hello… they are still obviously the best choice. They have to get a new car or house on a regular basis because it is practically expected. Someone who has attained the level of greatness that they have must always have the newest and best. Let's all take a moment of silence now just to remember and be thankful for all of the wonderful people that we know who fit this mold. Warm…fuzzy thoughts, right?

Of course I've adopted quite a sarcastic tone at this point, but seriously, you know what I'm talking about, don't you? We really all have met that person. And honestly, we are all just a little bit annoyed at that person, aren't we? Even people who are like that are frustrated and perturbed with people who seem to live with a sense of entitlement! Unfortunately though, the truth is that we are all susceptible to potentially falling into this slightly overdeveloped image of ourselves. It is of the utmost importance that we do not allow ourselves to be entrapped by this mind-set, however, because it becomes impossible to be content when we view the world as beholden to our existence.

What exactly is it that we deserve? Nothing. No, really…nothing. Everything we have is directly due to the goodness of God alone. *"And said, Naked came I out of my mother's womb, and naked shall I return thither: the Lord gave, and the Lord hath taken away; blessed be the name of the Lord."* (Job 1:21) Grasping the truth of that verse makes it incredibly easier to embrace the hardships of our life. We don't deserve health. We don't deserve financial independence. We don't deserve our material possessions. The perspective that Job gives in this verse is exactly what we need when we are faced with a difficulty or a loss in life.

Because of my arthritis, I can't run or jump anymore. I used to be able to perform those simplest of activities, but I cannot any longer. I used to be able to bend my wrists and ankles. Those simplest of motions are no longer possible for my body. It is hard sometimes to sit and think about what I used to be able to accomplish that I no longer can. Perhaps you have a similar example in your own life. Maybe you have lost something much more important than the flexibility of a joint. Just the thought of never having something or someone again can be very difficult to deal with emotionally. The only way to escape the imminent depression and regret that wants to flood into our hearts and minds is to develop a meek and lowly spirit. This is directly opposite of what the world would encourage you to do.

Humanistic philosophy says that when you have lost something, you should build yourself up through self-motivation and praise. You should just tell yourself how amazing you are and continue to reinforce a positive self-image. But if that doesn't work for you (and it won't, of course), then you can always try the Biblical approach to developing a contented outlook on life: *"the Lord gave, and the Lord hath taken away; blessed be the name of the Lord."* God gave me the ability to run…He took away that capability. Blessed be the name of the Lord! God provided me with the strength to jump at one point; then He removed that ability. Blessed be the name of the Lord! At one point, He provided me with the flexibility to bend my wrists and ankles, but one day God decided to change that. Blessed be the name of the Lord! A meek and lowly heart, mind, and spirit is absolutely critical in cultivating a contented perspective when it comes to the suffering and troubles that we endure.

I truly believe that begging God to change our mind-set, to help us to recognize His presence and provision, as well as to develop a lowly heart and spirit will allow every one of us to live such a more satisfied and contented life. A contented life will unleash new and exciting opportunities in our life. It will allow us to embrace the challenges and difficulties of our life because we realize that everything we have is a direct result of the goodness of a God Who longs for nothing but our best and continued growth in Him.

There are several other very tangible benefits to leading a contented life, however. This is such an important part of this book. I don't want to just tell you how the Bible says to live because it's the right thing to do. I also want to inspire you to accept, embrace, and use your weaknesses because I truly believe that contentment will make your life so much easier and happier. There are such tremendous advantages! Let us quickly look at some of the multiple blessings that will stem from developing a life full of contentment and satisfaction.

Contentment Brings Peace

"The LORD *will give strength unto his people; the* LORD *will bless his people with peace."* (Psalm 29:11) We see from the Word of God that peace is an emotion that He wants to give and will give to His children. As we have already seen, the difficulties of our life are so often used by God to bestow upon us just such a blessing as peace. I have found in my own life that my arthritis has helped me to be peacefully content. There are so many things that I cannot accomplish because of my arthritis that I have found I am much more content with the things that I can do. For example, as I mentioned previously, I can hardly run because of my arthritis, and even if I do "run," it is about as fast as a tortoise. But hey, slow and steady wins the race, right?

I remember once I actually lost a race to a seven-year old girl who was wearing a dress! Did I mention that humility is a virtue that stems from a physical ailment? People ask me sometimes if I'm angry because I can't run. No! I'm just thrilled that I can walk! Now I'm not going to lie and say that I never get frustrated or disappointed because of my arthritis. There have been times when I have gotten temporarily upset because I found out that I couldn't do something that I thought I would be able to do. This really doesn't happen that often though. As a rule, I don't get angry because of not being able to do something. I have that attitude because my arthritis has helped me to be content. That contentment then in turn allows me to be at peace with whatever circumstances or situations that come my way.

When a Christian takes the necessary steps to cultivate contentment in his life, he also simultaneously opens the doorway to a life full of peace and serenity. And isn't that a wonderful thought? Imagine a life where you are content and therefore at peace with whatever happens. You don't have to get so stressed and concerned. You could actually…gasp…relax. That's the life that God wants each of His children to live. He wants to give us peace. He wants to give us contentment. Peace is one of the immediate blessings that will envelop and overwhelm our lives as soon as we allow God to make us content with the pain and trials that we endure.

Contentment Brings Stability

Life is crazy! Have you noticed that? Everyone is busy, and everything seems to stay in a constant state of motion. There is no time to slow down. Absolutely no time can be allotted for relaxation or contemplation—no chances to take a step back and focus on what really matters. We live life in the fast lane. We aren't really going anywhere in particular, but we have to keep moving. Early mornings, late nights, and excessive amounts of caffeinated beverages have become the norm and practically the necessary. Text messaging, Wi-Fi Internet, and laptops are all essential telecommunication devices. People use their cell phones as if they literally provided oxygen.

When did our culture reach this point? When was apple pie replaced by power bars? When was cold cherry Coke replaced by a vanilla latte? When was going fishing on Saturday crowded out by overtime at the office? I have a theory about all of this change. I think that possibly our entire culture shifted one day when everyone became…unstable. Face it—a lot of people have just lost it. We live in a world defined by chaos and instability. People skip around to churches, continually searching for what they perceive as perfection. Men and women jump from job to job, looking for the ideal situation that will never come to fruition. People are always looking, searching, seeking.

Stability seems to be somewhat of a foreign concept at this point in our world's history. The root cause of instability, however, is very simply a lack of contentment. A contented person who is satisfied with his situation in life has such a greater opportunity to become solid, dependable, and stable. Once we become content with the pain and difficulties of life, we also develop a life of stability that will produce tangible benefits in every aspect of our life. Stability makes a person a better family member, a more attractive employee, a more respected church parishioner, and a more loved and dependable friend. Stop the chaos! Become contented with whatever challenges God has given to you and reap the benefit of a life full of stability and calm.

Contentment Brings Happiness

A contented and satisfied person is a much happier person indeed. People who are content with their life, limitations, societal status, and physical features are actually able to accomplish more in their life because they don't have to worry about reaching lofty heights or attaining a certain status. Now, there is certainly nothing wrong with being goal-oriented and driven to accomplish something, as long as it is a Christlike endeavor. However, to be focused upon such insignificant possessions such as cars, or things such as promotions, and similar items is simply unwise. Again, I think the biggest way that contentment brings about happiness is simply by changing our perspective and expectations.

Being a teenager, I get a firsthand glimpse of how preoccupied so many people are with how they look. My mom was recently telling me about two girls with whom I am friends who admit that they take over two and a half hours to get ready every morning. Wow! I don't care how good you look after you're done; that's just not worth it. I like sleeping too much. Usually girls get too much of the burden, but these days guys are unfortunately just as bad. Everywhere you look there are styled haircuts, jewelry, and the latest fashions adorning guys. I'm not a big fan of fashion trends myself, but it is simply an outward display of a group of people's wanting to be attractive to others. Overall, our entire culture is obsessed with how they look.

It also seems like an increasingly high number of people are spending insane amounts of money to keep up their appearance. Whether it is an expensive surgery, a constantly evolving wardrobe, or endless accessories, people are more and more apt these days to pull out their wallet in order to "look good."

Now there are two questions I want to rhetorically ask.

- First of all, does bankrupting yourself in a vain attempt to look good really make anyone happy? I'm guessing the answer is no.
- Secondly, what prompts someone to go to such lengths to improve his or her cosmetic appeal?

The answer to these questions is quite simple: a lack of contentment is the precursor to such behavior. The bottom line is that nobody can ever be truly happy until he learns to be content. Conversely, someone who is content with his looks, his possessions, and his limitations has the power to allow a complete happiness to overwhelm his life. When we take a contented mind-set into our day-to-day activities, we not only allow ourselves to be able to embrace the difficulties that present themselves, but also open the door for unprecedented happiness and satisfaction. It's a win-win situation! The subjects of happiness and joy are covered in depth in the next chapter, but for now let it resonate in your heart that contentment is an absolutely essential virtue if you want to live a life devoid of depression and full of satisfaction.

When I think about contentment, I am forever reminded of Jesus and His example of a truly sacrificially content person. He was content to leave the glories of Heaven to suffer for sins that He never committed. He was content to be persecuted for the sake of others. He was content to live in a state of human want while on earth. Think about it for a moment. People complain about missing out on a promotion or not being able to afford a new car or vacation while Jesus didn't have a place to lay His head at night. *"And Jesus saith unto him, The foxes have holes, and the birds of the air have nests; but the Son of man hath not where to lay his head."* (Matthew 8:20) Think about how much you value home. For most, home is a place of rest, peace, and comfort. Imagine not having one at all. It would be very difficult to be content without the basic necessity of a house in which to live. It would be impossible for us to be content with such a situation if we had the power to change our circumstances. Would you be able to live on earth without a dwelling place when you possessed the ability to live in the nicest, most expensive, luxurious house possible? I wouldn't. Yet that is exactly what Christ did. He was content to live in such circumstances because He saw the greater good that would be accomplished.

In order to embrace our challenges and weaknesses, we must follow Christ's example in contentment. I Peter 2:21-23 says,

"For even hereunto were ye called: because Christ also suffered for us, leaving us an example, that ye should follow his steps: [22]Who did no sin, neither was guile found in his mouth: [23]Who, when he

*was reviled, reviled not again; when he suffered, he threatened
not; but committed himself to him that judgeth righteously."*
Jesus suffered more than any of the rest of us ever will, and He suffered
contentedly. He left us an example that should be followed.

I truly believe that if we were to cultivate a perpetually content spirit,
it would absolutely revolutionize the way that we live our life. It would
change our perspective on hardship. It would make bearable the unbearable. It would make tolerable the intolerable. It would change everything
if we were just simply content with the life that God has given to us. I
promise, if you will be *"content with such things as ye have,"* you will reap
the blessings of peace, stability, and happiness.

We are all presented with difficulties that we must face in our lifetime. And often how we choose to handle these limitations or trials becomes the defining aspect of who we are. Contentment plays such a huge
role in this reaction to trouble or pain. Can we say like Paul in II Timothy
4:7, *"I have fought a good fight, I have finished my course, I have kept the
faith"?* What contentment is personified in this verse! Looking back on
his life, Paul reflects upon the fact that he has done everything he can.
He is content. He has fought the good fight, finished his course, and kept
the faith. Now it is up to us to do the same. *"Fight the good fight of faith,
lay hold on eternal life, whereunto thou art also called, and hast professed
a good profession before many witnesses."* (I Timothy 6:12)

"*Most of the grand truths of God have to be learned by trouble; they must be burned into us by the hot iron of affliction, otherwise we shall not truly receive them.*"

– *Charles H. Spurgeon*

CHAPTER SEVEN

THE BEST DAY OF MY LIFE

Living Life for Everything It's Worth

Have you ever paid attention to the various ways that people answer the common question "How are you doing today?" I think that you can tell a lot about a person and his outlook on life by his response to this simple question. The person who quickly answers "Fine" is probably a very busy person who thinks it's a waste of time or a mere formality to exchange greetings with a fellow man. Someone who tells you that he "Can't complain" is most likely a satisfied person, not overwhelmingly happy, not unusually upset. Every once in a while, though, you will have the pleasure of meeting a person who responds in such a way that you know that he is a joy-filled person.

My granddad will tell you that he's "So good that if he was any better he'd have to be twins just to stand himself." That reply sounds joyful to me! My dad will tell you that he is "Outstanding!" You can pretty much rest assured that a depressed man would not use this word. What is my personal response to this question? I usually tell people that "Today's the best day of my life!"

I think that lets people know from the start of our conversation that I love my life. My response lets people know that I'm not upset, angry, depressed, or anxious. I'm having the best day of my life! By the way, let me give you my word on it—I do love my life. I wouldn't trade places with anyone else in the world, and I mean that. I have an awesome family, awesome friends, an awesome church, and most of all, an awesome Saviour!

A lot of people, maybe even most people, aren't happy with their lives though. Again, I see this over and over again in the lives of other teenagers. I hate to say it, but I don't think I'm exaggerating to say that at least 50 percent of the teenagers whom I meet are depressed, angry, frustrated, confused, anxious, insecure, and bitter. I read just a few days ago that suicide is the third leading cause of death in people between the ages of 10 to 24 years old. Suicide. It boggles my mind to think that someone could ever find himself in such a hopeless situation or set of circumstances that he would consider taking his own life. It happens though. It happens all the time. It happens way too much.

The Bible makes it clear that God wants us all to have the joy of Christ in our lives. The Bible tells us Who is the Giver of our joy in Romans 15:13 which says, *"Now the God of hope fill you with all joy and peace in believing, that ye may abound in hope, through the power of the Holy Ghost."* The God of hope is the One Who gives us joy and peace. God does not want His children to be depressed! God knows the adverse affect that it will have upon us as His children, but He also knows the adverse affect that our miserable state will have on the people around us—especially the unsaved. Think about how terribly it hurts our soul-winning efforts if we do not have the joy of Christ in our lives. How many people do you think would get saved from the following pitch to an unsaved person? "Hi, my name is David McCroskey. I'm a completely miserable Christian who hates his life. Would you like to become a Christian, too?" Yeah, that message would hook a ton of converts, wouldn't it? Now of course one could argue that a soul winner would never actually use that terminology when witnessing to a person. My contention is that you can't hide it if you aren't happy, though! People can tell if you are excited about being a Christian or if you are so busy with your life that living the Christian life is an afterthought to you. It's really that simple.

Furthermore, living a joyful life is absolutely essential when it comes to accepting, embracing, and finally using the difficulties of our life. During this segment of the book, the focus has been on on embracing our challenges and weaknesses. All is futile, however, if we never embrace life itself. We will never be able to love the trials and tribulations of our life until we love life. It's a wonderful life. It really is! Take my word for it if you don't believe it yourself. The purpose of this chapter is cut and dried. I want you to love your life. I want you to fall in love with the God Who gave you your life. I want you to love your difficulties. I want you to realize that a part of what makes up the crazy, unpredictable, beautiful disaster that we call "life" is the difficulty that lies in our path.

I believe I'm pretty much the happiest person that you could meet. I'm nauseatingly happy. Unfortunately, there are people who literally cannot be around me very long because they cannot stand how happy I am. I mean, I'm thrilled! I randomly let out a somewhat uncontrollably and potentially terrifying yell just because it hits me one more time how excited I am to be alive and living the amazing life that I do. As I stated earlier, I wouldn't trade lives with anyone else. Bill Gates can have his money. Oprah Winfrey can have her influence. Lebron James can have his athleticism. I'll take the life that God has given me any day of the week. I wake up smiling every morning because I'm looking forward with great expectation to the wonderful day that I know I'm about to experience. I'm enthusiastic and exuberant practically to a fault. I'm unashamedly, unabashedly, and unadulteratedly happy.

A while back a friend of mine asked me to write down ten things that I thought made me as happy as I am. As I sat down and wrote out what he had asked for, I began to realize that there were no secrets to happiness. Being joyful is all about little things. It's all about a tiny attitude adjustment here and a shift in focus there. It's about noticing things that most people don't care to realize. It's about recognizing the immense blessings that God has given to us. No magical concoction. No mystical potion. Just a compilation of very simple ideas form the basis for a lifetime of true joy. With that said…here's the list.

Salvation

As I mentioned in chapter one, on January 8, 1997, I accepted Jesus Christ into my life as my personal Saviour. What an amazing day! I had heard the Gospel story more times than I could possibly begin to count, but it was not until January 8, 1997, that I asked Jesus to be my Saviour and knew that He had really entered into my life in a new context. Before that day, I had prayed the "sinner's prayer" many times, but I really don't think that I was ever saved until January 8. I had repeated words and gone through the motions, but it wasn't until that morning with my mom that I came to a point where I knew that I *needed* God and the salvation that only He could provide. The very thought of going to Hell scared the living daylights out of me, and there was a period of time when I would pray for salvation ritualistically. Every time I had a spare moment, I was asking God to give me a home in Heaven! It wasn't until my mom explained to me eternal security that I believe I finally *trusted* in Christ's sacrificial, substitutionary death.

I was so excited to know that I had finally gotten saved and that I was never going to have to worry about my eternal destination again! But the secret here is that I have never gotten over that feeling! I thank God every single day that He saved me, redeemed me, and reached way down for me! Old things are passed away; behold all things are become new! That's pretty exciting stuff! Have you ever thought about how a constant awareness of salvation would make it completely impossible to be sad or down for any length of time? How are we going to be upset about an item's breaking when we are thinking about God's giving us eternal life for absolutely nothing? If someone walked up to me on the street this afternoon and handed me $1,000, I wouldn't be happy and thankful for just a few minutes. I would be excited for a while! That's $1,000 that was just given to me! I didn't earn it. I didn't deserve it. I didn't trade for it. I just received. How much more should we be forever exhilarated at the thought of salvation?

When I was 15 years old, my granddad bought my sister and me a Jeep Grand Cherokee. Yeah…I was pretty happy. Okay, so maybe that's an understatement. I was thrilled actually! Because of my physical limitations and some legal issues revolving around my medical situation, I had never been able to work a steady job. I worked as much as I possibly could—but it was never enough to have a legitimate chance at being able to purchase a car in high school. Now I have never been the kind of teenage guy whose entire life revolved around four spinning wheels, but of course I wanted a vehicle that would provide me with a certain level of independence as I grew older. I remember how happy I was when I first learned that a car had been provided for me! I was so thankful and so joyful. I still am. Almost every time I sit down behind the steering wheel, I try to remind myself of how grateful I should be for such an undeserved blessing.

How much more important is salvation than a car? I love to hear people thank God for their salvation when they are praying. To me, their words are just some of the sweetest that I have ever heard. That tells me that they haven't gotten over it. They don't take the gift of God for granted. We were so undeserving.

> "But God commendeth his love toward us, in that, while we were yet sinners, Christ died for us. ⁹Much more then, being now justified by his blood, we shall be saved from wrath through him. ¹⁰For if, when we were enemies, we were reconciled to God by the death of his Son, much more, being reconciled, we shall be saved by his life. ¹¹And not only so, but we also joy in God through our Lord Jesus Christ, by whom we have now received the atonement."
>
> (Romans 5:8-11)

God provided for our salvation while we were still nothing more than sinners. But now we are reconciled to Him through the death of His Son! And look back at the last sentence in the above-listed verses: *"we also joy in God through our Lord Jesus Christ, by whom we have now received the atonement."* Why should we be happy? Why should we be exceedingly joyful? Luke 10:20 gives us the answer: *"Notwithstanding in this rejoice not, that the spirits are subject unto you; but rather rejoice, because your names are written in heaven."* The number one reason why I'm so happy? I'm saved! I could spend this whole chapter addressing how wonderful God's gift of salvation is, but I would never be able to come close to describing how amazing salvation is. The Bible sums it up better than man could ever. II Corinthians 9:15 says, *"Thanks be unto God for his unspeakable gift."* Salvation is an unspeakable gift.

Fellowship With Believers

Through my church, I am surrounded by some of the Godliest people on the face of the planet. The caliber of people that I get to emulate through my interaction with them at my church is truly fantastic! Strong, dependable men have displayed loyalty and masculinity. Wonderful ladies have embodied a sweet and friendly spirit. There are teenagers with whom I can enjoy spending time and creating a lifetime worth of memories. Even outside of my church though, God has still provided me with exceptional friends. Many of my closest friends do not go to my church, but they are still incredibly good influences on my life. I thank God daily for surrounding me with the kind of people who will point me toward God instead of trying to destroy my faith in Christ. A good friend of mine recently sent me an email with a chapter of Bible verses that she was excited about and wanted to share with me. I thought as I read that email that I am so thankful I have friends who send me Bible verses.

You would probably be surprised if you heard some of the conversations that I have with my friends. We talk about our favorite preachers, our favorite sermons, and prayer requests that we'd like for the other to pray about—not exactly your average teenage conversation topics. I thank God that He has given me an opportunity to fellowship with and to be friends with people who exalt Christ in their lives. Sometimes the fellowship that we have with those around us is one of the few things that keeps us holding on.

Quite often the Apostle Paul relied on his fellow believers to help him through a troublesome time period. In Philippians 1:3-5 Paul writes, *"I thank my God upon every remembrance of you, Always in every prayer of mine for you all making request with joy, For your fellowship in the gospel from the first day until now."* Every time that Paul even thought about these people, he was immediately joyful. What a tremendous blessing! There are people in my life as well who prompt instant happiness every time they are brought to my mind.

Friends are such an integral part of life. Are they the most important part of life? Certainly not! Can they become destructive if they are the wrong kinds of influences? Of course they can. But if you are blessed enough to have the right kind of friends, then you are a blessed person indeed. Even if you only have one true friend in life, you possess something that many never will. Oftentimes there are people who go an entire lifetime without ever finding that one person they can completely trust and upon whom they can depend. Probably the most popular and appropriate example of friendship in the Bible is demonstrated between David and Jonathan. The Scripture makes it clear that they had a bond that very few friends ever attain.

> *"And it came to pass, when he had made an end of speaking unto Saul, that the soul of Jonathan was knit with the soul of David, and Jonathan loved him as his own soul.* [2]*And Saul took him that day, and would let him go no more home to his father's house.* [3]*Then Jonathan and David made a covenant, because he loved him as his own soul.* [4]*And Jonathan stripped himself of the robe that was upon him, and gave it to David, and his garments, even to his sword, and to his bow, and to his girdle."* (I Samuel 18:1-4)

What David and Jonathan had between the two of them was something special. Very few people ever get to experience the kind of devotion that was apparently shared between these two men. Of course we know that Jonathan, at one point, went to great lengths to save David's life. Later on when David was king, he returned the favor to Jonathan by helping Mephiboseth. *"And David said, Is there yet any that is left of the house of Saul, that I may shew him kindness for Jonathan's sake?"* (II Samuel 9:1) The mighty king of Israel showed kindness to a poor cripple because even after Jonathan was dead, David wanted to honor his friend. That is a true, never-dying friendship. That's the kind of friendship that makes life so enjoyable. It's one of the number-one reasons why I am so excited about my life. God has given me many friends who color the canvas of my life, and that thought makes me energetic and joyful about my wonderful life!

Be Happy for the Little Things

I woke up this morning…alive! But it only got better from there. I stumbled into the kitchen and made quite possibly the best cup of coffee that this world has ever seen. That made me happy—very happy! While I sipped on my coffee, I read through a few chapters in my Bible and reveled in the Word of God. From there I went to my computer and checked my emails. I had several very nice emails from good friends of mine who were wishing me well or just checking in to let me know what was happening. It's raining fairly hard outside right now. That's good for we desperately need the rain. In a few minutes I'm going to go grab some breakfast and take my morning medication. It's a comforting thought to know that I have food to eat and medicine to keep me healthy. I could enumerate exactly everything that I've done or thought about so far this morning, but that really isn't the point.

What is the point? No, I haven't lost my mind or run out of things to write about. I want you to notice something about my day so far. Nothing overtly exciting has happened. Basically, nothing out of the ordinary has occurred whatsoever—no million dollar windfalls, no free trips to Cancun, and so far certainly no chance of the Atlanta Braves winning the World Series! My day has thus far consisted of nothing but nice little occurrences, but nothing special. Here is what you should know, however. As of right now (7:32 a.m.), I am in an absolutely impenetrably good mood! I'm so happy right now I can hardly stand being around myself! That's just the honest truth.

I get really, really excited about the little things of life. It will tremendously improve your outlook on life if you will on purpose notice the amazing little blessings that God is constantly raining down upon us. My dad often tells about how he very regularly prays when he wakes up in the morning that he will have hot water when he takes a shower. That seems like such a small thing, doesn't it? Why would you bother to even think about whether or not you are going to have hot water when you take your morning shower? Well, have you ever taken a freezing cold shower? It has a tendency not to be such a pleasant experience. In fact, for some people it would completely ruin their day before it ever really got started. So why not go ahead and ask God for hot water? Yes, it's a small, seemingly insignificant request, but it's not as if God doesn't care. He does. And then when you turn on the faucet and hot water pours out, thank God for that! Be excited about that!

We take so many blessings in life for granted. And let me say this, why do we get so angry when things go wrong but never think twice when things go right? We get so upset when the car doesn't start, but we don't get really happy the majority of the time when it starts right up. That's a shame! And also, we worry so much about things that never happen, but we are never thankful for what doesn't occur. Think about it. How much emotional energy do we waste worrying and stressing over things that never end up happening? But when was the last time that you were excited because something bad didn't happen? Have you ever gotten home from work and smiled because you didn't get fired or laid off? Have you ever driven to a friend's house and been upbeat because you didn't get in a car accident? People don't think like that. People don't have that perspective on life.

Acts 14:17 says, *"Nevertheless he left not himself without witness, in that he did good, and gave us rain from heaven, and fruitful seasons, filling our hearts with food and gladness."* When was the last time you were joyful over the rain that God sent to your town? How about the last time you thanked Him for the sunshine? Electricity? Indoor plumbing? Listen, if you can't be happy about indoor plumbing then there just isn't a whole lot of hope for you. We've got to start getting excited about the little things in life. It will completely revolutionize your life. It will keep a smile on your face—no matter what trial or trouble you are enduring. I promise you. Now stop right now and thank God for indoor plumbing!

Rejoice in God's Love

One of the most exciting things that ever happens in my life is seeing God working. Whether it's an answered prayer, the changing of some less-than-favorable circumstance, or grace to make it through a difficult situation, it always excites me to see God flexing His muscle in my life. God is so adept at helping His children when they are at their weakest points, and a person with physical pain like myself has a lot of weak points. It should absolutely fill our hearts with joy as Christians when we see our Saviour and Creator doing something amazing in our lives. Omniscient, omnipresent, omnipotent God takes enough interest in our life to actively be a part of it. That thought makes me joyful!

Have you ever really sat back and fully contemplated the love that God has for you? I mean, we're talking about God here—God, the Creator of the universe; God, the most powerful Being imaginable; God, perfection embodied. He loves you. He loves you so much that He sacrificed His only Son to die a horrible death so that He could be reunited with you one day in Heaven. He thinks about you. He watches out for you. He blesses you and keeps you safe. Look at what the Bible says about the love of God.

Sacrificial Love

"I am crucified with Christ: nevertheless I live; yet not I, but Christ liveth in me: and the life which I now live in the flesh I live by the faith of the Son of God, who loved me, and gave himself for me." (Galatians 2:20)

Inseparable Love

"Who shall separate us from the love of Christ? shall tribulation, or distress, or persecution, or famine, or nakedness, or peril, or sword? 38For I am persuaded, that neither death, nor life, nor angels, nor principalities, nor powers, nor things present, nor things to come, 39Nor height, nor depth, nor any other creature, shall be able to separate us from the love of God, which is in Christ Jesus our Lord." (Romans 8:35, 38, 39)

Greatest Love

"This is my commandment, That ye love one another, as I have loved you. Greater love hath no man than this, that a man lay down his life for his friends." (John 15:12, 13)

Comforting Love

"Now our Lord Jesus Christ himself, and God, even our Father, which hath loved us, and hath given us everlasting consolation and good hope through grace." (II Thessalonians 2:16)

Defining Love

"He that loveth not knoweth not God: for God is love."

(I John 4:8)

Inexplicable Love

"Behold, what manner of love the Father hath bestowed upon us, that we should be called the sons of God: therefore the world knoweth us not, because it knew him not." (I John 3:1)

Great Love

"But God, who is rich in mercy, for his great love wherewith he loved us." (Ephesians 2:4)

Incomprehensible Love

"And to know the love of Christ, which passeth knowledge, that ye might be filled with all the fulness of God." (Ephesians 3:19)

Everlasting Love

"The LORD *hath appeared of old unto me, saying, Yea, I have loved thee with an everlasting love: therefore with lovingkindness have I drawn thee."* (Jeremiah 31:3)

Thoughtful Love

"What is man, that thou art mindful of him? and the son of man, that thou visitest him? For thou hast made him a little lower than the angels, and hast crowned him with glory and honour." (Psalm 8:4, 5)

Living with the constant awareness of the undeniable love of God will change your attitude perhaps faster than anything else. It's mind-boggling that such Majesty could care about you and me. But He does—and that knowledge makes me happy!

Focus on the Positive

All is never lost. No, really, it's true. There will never come a point in your life where there is absolutely nothing about which you can be happy. It's not possible, and it will never happen. There is always going to be light at the end of the tunnel. There is always a rainbow after the storm. There is a silver lining in the clouds. I know that there are times in life when it seems like nothing is going right. The truth is not that everything is going wrong, however. The truth is that we are so blinded by what is going wrong that we can no longer see the wonderful blessings that are continuing to inundate us. There are times when it is simply too hard for people to focus on the positive—not because the positive isn't there but because it is crowded out by the pain and misery that they are feeling at the time.

I have already touched on this concept, but I really believe it is necessary to stress the importance of focusing on the positives. We get so bogged down in our difficulties, and instead of giving those difficulties to God and allowing Him to work through our situation, we allow that challenge to become the all-consuming focus of our life. Sometimes we just have to forget about things for a little while. It's a much better use of our energy to think and dwell on the great things in our life than to worry and stress over the inevitable negatives. What is one of the reasons that I am so incredibly happy in my life? Because I try to just let things go and don't worry about the negative or unfortunate circumstances in which I sometimes find myself. I focus on the positive and enjoy my life so much more!

Be Around Happy People

There are basically two types of people in life:

- Happy people
- Not-so-happy people

I shared about how my great-grandmother was not such a pleasant lady all of the time. You've probably known someone like my great-grandmother. My dad was always enduringly kind to my great-grandmother and tried as hard as he could to cheer her up whenever he was around. But my dad has a very unique personality, and he is great at cheering up depressed people. Most of us react to people like my great-grandmother by avoiding them. And I can't honestly say that avoiding a chronically upset person is a bad choice.

Of course, as Christians it is our responsibility to be kind and compassionate toward everyone, but when someone is beginning to negatively influence us, then I think it is only wise to distance ourselves from that person. We all know how certain kinds of people influence us for either righteousness or unrighteousness. David and Jonathan influenced each other for good, whereas Jonadab influenced Amnon for great evil. How are the people in your life influencing you?

I was just talking to a friend of mine a few days ago about how different friends seem to make us want to do different things. My friend was telling me that she loses her temper faster if she is around a certain person whom we both know. I responded that conversely another one of our mutual friends always made me feel more relaxed and comfortable than anyone else. Our emotions and moods are oftentimes largely dependent upon those around us.

So what can sometimes be the answer to our own despondent attitude? Quite simply, to surround ourselves with excited, upbeat people. This is one of the methods that I use to keep myself so happy all of the time. If I am starting to feel a little bit down throughout the day, there are certain friends that I do not contact. It's not that I don't like them. In fact, some of my absolute favorite people in the world are on that mental list of people that I try to avoid when I'm feeling sad. They are fantastic people, but they do not often lift me up from a bad mood. Conversely, there are certain people that I always try to talk to when I'm upset. There is one person in particular who seems to always know how to brighten my day. I try to surround myself with people who speak encouraging and uplifting words. It helps keep me focused on the positives of life and allows me more fully to embrace the difficulty that I may be dealing with at the time.

Look around yourself. How are the people with whom you spend time influencing your outlook and attitude? Are they making you happier and more filled with the joy of Christ, or are they dragging you down into the depths of depression and self-pity? You will never be able to be happy about the struggles that God has placed in your life until you are able to be excited about the life in general that He has given you. And you will never be able to be happy about your life if you are continually allowing your spirit to be influenced by people who do not share the same joy and excitement that you want in your own life.

Be Excited . . . Always

*"Great is my boldness of speech toward you, great is my glorying of you: I am filled with comfort, I am **exceeding joyful** in all our tribulation."* (II Corinthians 7:4) Exceeding joyful? For many people, those words don't even have meaning anymore. The thought of being joyful doesn't seem possible. Exceeding joyful? Not a chance. Are you there? Are you walking through life in nothing more than a functioning coma? Can you remember the last time that you laughed so hard that it literally hurt

physically? When was the last time you went for hours without worrying about pain or sorrow? A lot of people can't recall those times.

It's well documented in the Bible that Paul had quite a difficult life. Nothing really ever seemed to happen easily for him. Everywhere he went and everything that he did seemed to involve a beating, or imprisonment, or a near-death experience. And yet we see in II Corinthians 7:4 that he was not just happy…not just joyful…but exceedingly so! How did he reach that point?

I believe you find part of the answer in the beginning of the verse: *"Great is my boldness…."* I think Paul was an excited person. I think he was high-energy, always going somewhere and doing something. He was obviously an active man who kept plenty busy. I think part of the "secret" to being a very happy person is just to attack life.

Just try it. Wake up in the morning excited about the day. Don't wake up and think about everything that you have to get done. Don't think about work, or the bills, or the deadlines that must be met. Think to yourself that this is one more day where you get to experience the amazing and awesome blessings of life on God's great earth! You can ask my family, and they will tell you that when I get up in the morning, I am immediately excited. I go around and find everyone in the house and tell them, "Hey! This is going to be a great day!" Why? Because it is going to be a great day! I have no doubts in my mind. I expect that there are fantastic things that God wants to do with the day, or He wouldn't have given it to me. Challenge yourself. Get happy. Get excited. Smile. Let God fill your heart with unspeakable joy! *"Whom having not seen, ye love; in whom, though now ye see him not, yet believing, ye rejoice with joy unspeakable and full of glory."* (I Peter 1:8)

Be Obedient to God

"Blessed is every one that feareth the LORD; that walketh in his ways. For thou shalt eat the labour of thine hands: happy shalt thou be, and it shall be well with thee." (Psalm 128:1, 2) Of course, I wish I could tell you that I've always followed and obeyed God, and therefore I am always happy. Of course that would not be a true statement. We all drift and

stray from the love of God at some point or another, and everyone even directly disobeys Him from time to time. And all of us know the instant regret and unhappiness that floods our soul when we know we've grieved the Spirit of God inside of us. The Bible clearly teaches that one of the best ways to increase our joy is to simply obey the Lord.

God wants us to be happy. That's such a simple, yet sometimes neglected truth. It's absolutely true, though. The Bible even gives us ways to increase the level of our joy. John 16:24 says, *"Hitherto have ye asked nothing in my name: ask, and ye shall receive, that your joy may be full."* God has outlined certain ways that we can increase our joy and happiness through our interaction with Him. Praying and asking for the blessings of God is one "sure-fire" way to increase our joy. In the same way, obedience to God is absolutely essential in order for the Christian to lead a life full of happiness. Many entire books have been devoted to this issue of obedience to God, but I thought it was important to put it on the list that I gave to my friend. It really is a major part of being joy-filled.

If we never get to the point where we are consistently and quickly submitting to God, then neither will we ever reach the point where we can embrace the trials and difficulties in our life. You will never be capable of accepting, embracing, or using your challenges and weaknesses if you are not willing to do the simple things that you know God has instructed you to do.

Read God's Word

I'll just be honest with you. I used to struggle immensely with reading my Bible on a regular basis. For some reason, the Bible had this great intimidation factor to it. I felt like I had to block out great amounts of time in my day to devote solely to reading the Bible, and of course, that just never seemed to happen. It was years after I became a Christian before I could finally say that I had read the entire Bible. But even after I had read the Bible from "cover to cover," I still seemed to have a hard time establishing any kind of reliable schedule for reading my Bible on a daily basis. It was not until I heard a sermon one night at a Christian camp that my whole attitude toward the Word of God was altered.

I was 15 years old, and I guess it would only be fair to admit that I had really started to get interested in girls. Now, I've never been a very shy person, and the truth is that I can vividly remember the first time that I had a "crush" on a girl. I was all of eight years old. At the age when most guys still think girls have "cooties," I was planning my proposal to the cute blonde in my Sunday school class. But of course things became more serious the further along I traveled in my teenage years, and I was beginning to reach that point where girls were beginning to occupy more and more of my time. The preacher at camp that night really tied together a thought that made me think about my Bible in a completely different way.

He started to talk about guy/girl relationships and how dating couples often exchange notes and letters with each other, telling one another how much they care. He told how he would read his fiancée's love letters over and over again. He shared how excited he was every time he sat down to read one of her notes. He loved those notes so much because he knew how much the author loved him. It wasn't intimidating to read the letters. It wasn't a burden to him. He loved it! He looked forward to her notes and letters with great anticipation! Well, I had received a couple of notes from girls, and I was definitely agreeing with everything that the preacher was saying. I knew the excitement that I felt as I opened a letter from a girl who I thought was attractive and sweet. But then the preacher tied the thought of a love letter to the Bible, and the comparison finally clicked in my mind.

I realized the Bible was written as a letter to me from Someone Who loved me more than any girl here on earth ever could. And He didn't just write down how He felt about me, but He also took the time to give me instructions and precepts that would help guide me through life. He also sprinkled in encouraging and inspirational words for me to draw strength from while I went through the dark times that He knew would come. "How utterly amazing!" I thought. Suddenly, I wasn't intimidated by the Bible anymore. I didn't feel pressured to read it; I just wanted to.

Next to salvation, the Word of God is arguable the greatest gift that has been given to mankind. It is such an unbelievably amazing Book! No other book in history has been so loved and cherished as the Bible. Conversely, no other book in history has been so hated and despised as the Bible. People have fought desperately to possess the Bible. People have fought desperately to destroy it. It's the number-one-selling Book of all time. It's the oldest, most revolutionary, controversial, and polarizing Book ever to be written.

"The grass withereth, the flower fadeth: but the word of our God shall stand for ever." (Isaiah 40:8)

"For ever, O LORD, thy word is settled in heaven." (Psalm 119:89)

"But the word of the Lord endureth for ever. And this is the word which by the gospel is preached unto you." (I Peter 1:25)

I once remember reading a quote from Sir Walter Scott where he said, "There is but one book: the Bible." It's that simple. No other book can even come close to comparing to the wonderful, perfect Word of God. The Bible in a Christian's life should not just bring comfort and strength, but also an immense amount of joy. *"Thy words were found, and I did eat them; and thy word was unto me the joy and rejoicing of mine heart: for I am called by thy name, O LORD God of hosts."* (Jeremiah 15:16) Immerse yourself in the Word of God...and rejoice!

Live Like You're Dying

I was almost afraid to include this last item on the list because I'm afraid that many people consider this to be a humanistic, worldly philosophy. But I really don't think that it is. In James the Bible addresses how we should live our life with a constant awareness that we may not have another day to live. *"Whereas ye know not what shall be on the morrow. For what is your life? It is even a vapour, that appeareth for a little time, and then vanisheth away."* (James 4:14)

Life flies by. I'm realizing that truth more and more the older I get. When I was younger, it seemed like days would drag on and on. Now however, it seems like I turn around and a year has passed. I can't explain why that is, but I'm definitely becoming more and more aware of the fact that there is only so much life to be lived. I find, though, that most people don't live with that mind-set.

We live in a very carefree world. Nobody seemingly cares what anyone does, and it doesn't matter anyway because there is always tomorrow to make up for things. That's the attitude that many adopt. I have known of people who ruined their reputation for a lifetime because of a stupid deed that they did without thought for tomorrow. Now, I know that some of you may be thinking that I'm advocating such a carefree attitude because of the subtitle to this portion of the chapter. Let me assure you that nothing could be further from the truth. What I'm trying to convey is not a reckless abandon, but rather a focused mind-set based upon the knowledge that we may not have tomorrow.

It is so important to live life with an "all-out" mentality. I have a very good friend who is famous for just attacking whatever it is that he is doing at the time. On the soccer field, he runs circles around everyone else. When we play pickup football, he is always the kid who ends up bleeding before things are over. Sometimes people like him are looked down upon as reckless and cavalier, but I admire him. He gives everything he has to whatever it is that he's doing. He has taken to heart, *"Whatsoever thy hand findeth to do, do it with thy might...."* (Ecclesiastes 9:10) Let me encourage you to live your life the same way that my friend does. It will make quite a difference in your attitude and ability to deal with the trials and hardships that come your way.

Smile like it's the last chance you have to show the world your heart. Embrace your loved one as if it's the last time you'll ever hold that person in your arms. Laugh like you might never get to again. Love like it could all end tomorrow. Live like it's the last breath you may take. *"Whether therefore ye eat, or drink, or whatsoever ye do, do all to the glory of God."* (I Corinthians 10:31) Don't leave regrets. Don't wonder "What if?" Don't question. Just do everything you can today and take full advantage of every opportunity that comes your way. Make a difference while you still can. Be happy. Be excited!

There is such a lack of true, God-given joy in the world today that it is truly refreshing when you meet a person who is filled with the joy of Christ—the kind of people who tell you they're "So good, if they were any better they'd have to be twins just to stand themselves!" These are the kind of people who make our lives just a little bit more livable. I pray that you are one of these people. Go ahead, let God fill your life with His irrepressible joy, and make today the best day of your life!

"This is the day which the LORD hath made; we will rejoice and be glad in it." (Psalm 118:24)

"*I thank God for my handicaps,
for through them,
I have found myself,
my work, and my God.*"

– Helen Keller

CHAPTER EIGHT

I Wouldn't Change a Thing

Being Thankful for the Difficulties of Life

I suppose that everyone has certain little pet peeves that just annoy them more than they should let them bother them. I have things like that as well. For me, one of the number one things that rubs me the wrong way is when someone doesn't say, "Thank you." It seems like such a simple phrase to say. It's not long. It's not complicated. But there are many people who apparently have a serious allergic reaction to having to utter those two simple words. I am thinking of a certain person right now, and I honestly do not think I have ever heard him say thank you. It's not because of a lack of opportunity. He has received many gifts and presents from the people around him, but he always just takes whatever is being handed to him without a word. I just think that it is quite regrettable that he has never been taught how to express gratitude properly.

I've been brought up by my parents to say thank you for anything and everything. If somebody gives me the flu, my natural reaction is to thank him profusely! And I find myself expressing gratitude and thankfulness often, because I am blessed with so many wonderful people around me who are always doing or saying nice things. I have a myriad of blessings for which to be thankful. I'm thankful for my parents who are such excellent role models. I'm thankful for my sisters, who are both lovely young ladies. I'm thankful for my brother, who is the coolest guy ever (and an absolutely incredible roommate). I'm grateful for my friends who keep me laughing and relaxed. I'm thankful for my church, my academic background, my car, and the future opportunities that I know are waiting for me. I could go on forever about the plethora of tremendous benefits for which I am thankful in my life.

You probably know what I'm about to say next, don't you? I've said it before, and I mean it. One of the things about my life for which I am the most thankful is all of the difficulties and medical problems that God has brought my way. Remember back in chapter four when I said that my goal for this part of the book was for you to thank God for whatever tragedies or challenges that He has given to you? Well, here we are. We've seen how He has created us uniquely and perfectly. We've seen the many blessings that stem directly from the afflictions that we've endured. We've looked at how to be content and joyful as we live out our days here on earth. Now it's time to wrap everything together and truly become genuinely thankful for what God has given to us.

Your Difficulty Is Part of You

I have already mentioned that I have always tried very hard to make sure that my physical limitations did not define who I am. When people think about me, I certainly do not want them to immediately think about my arthritis or my other medical situations. That would detract from my ability to glorify God through my life. But with that in mind, neither can I escape (or desire to escape) the fact that my physical trials are a part of who I am. They are a characterizing and distinguishing feature. God gave them to me. He obviously had a purpose in mind when He did that. It's my responsibility to embrace this gift from Him and cherish it as a part of my life forever.

Whatever you would consider your "cup" in life is also a part of you. But it's not just a part of you; it's a part of who you are. Somehow, in some way, that trial or that affliction has helped to shape the person that you have become. It has probably made you stronger. Maybe it has made you wiser. Perhaps you have become more dependent upon God and less sure of your own ability through the tests that you've endured. But no matter how you have come through the battle, you have been changed. You've been forever altered and affected because of what you have experienced. That difficulty is part of what makes you…you. Embrace that, my friend. Embrace the person that God has created you to be. Embrace the purpose that He had in mind when He mapped out and designed the events of your life. We have a tendency to reject what we would consider the "negative" circumstances of life, but the truth is that it is so much easier and wiser to accept and embrace them. God has refined us. He has used our weaknesses and limitations to mold us into a vessel that He then can use. *"Behold, I have refined thee, but not with silver; I have chosen thee in the furnace of affliction."* (Isaiah 48:10) To me that is exciting! Through the furnace of affliction, God has refined my life.

Let me add that God will always bring us through the furnace. I have addressed this already, but it's so true. Just like He delivered Shadrach, Meshach, and Abednego, God will save us as well. *"Now thanks be unto God, which always causeth us to triumph in Christ, and maketh manifest the savour of his knowledge by us in every place."* (II Corinthians 2:14) I don't know about you, but I know that the God of my creation and salvation is capable of making sure that I survive the trials and tribulations that He puts me through. As Paul points out in II Timothy 1:12, *"For the which cause I also suffer these things: nevertheless I am not ashamed: for I know whom I have believed, and am persuaded that he is able to keep that which I have committed unto him against that day."* There are things that we all must suffer through during our life. But we should never be ashamed or upset over those things because we know that the One Who placed us into the furnace of affliction not only can but will see us through to the other side. *"Being confident of this very thing, that he which hath begun a good work in you will perform it unto the day of Jesus Christ."* (Philippians 1:6)

God cares enough about you to take the time to plan out a detailed masterpiece that has become your life. And part of that design involves the necessary hardships that He, in this infinite knowledge and wisdom, knows will allow you to grow into the person the He created you to be. Whatever He placed into your life is a gift from your Father. It's part of you. Embrace it.

Your Difficulty Has Been for Your Good

When I was 11 years old, my neighbor who lived directly across the street from my house asked my dad if I would like to mow his lawn for the summer. Now stop and think about that proposition for a moment. I was 11 years old with severe, crippling juvenile rheumatoid arthritis. Not that I am now by any means a stout young man, but you should have seen me back then. At 11 I might have weighed all of 50 pounds. I mean I might have weighed 50 pounds if I was fully dressed and dripping wet. Physically speaking, I was definitely not cut out to be a yard man. Furthermore, remember that I live in Alabama. When our neighbor asked me to take care of his lawn for the "summer," he was referring to approximately 11 months of the year. So, of course, given all of these factors, my dad politely turned down our neighbor's proposal, right? Uh…not quite.

The truth is that I was excited about the opportunity, but I was very worried that I would not be able to handle the workload. I was now responsible for mowing, edging, and maintaining an entire yard for the summer. I had never before done anything like that, and I was quite scared that I was going to be physically incapable of performing this new job. And to be honest with you, there were plenty of times that summer when I was sure that I was right. It wasn't easy. Actually, it was quite hard.

More than one time, I stood behind that pushmower, completely exhausted, gripped with pain shooting through my knees and ankles, wondering how in the world I was going to take that next step. But I had two secret weapons in my arsenal, and both weapons came in the form of outside help. The first weapon was a God Who never ceases to amaze when it comes to somehow giving strength to those who need it. The second weapon was an amazing dad who way more than once would lay his hand on my shoulder and say, "Hey, Buddy, why don't you let me finish up this time?"

I got through that summer. In fact, I took care of that neighbor's yard (and several other people's yards as well) for many years. And what started out as a daunting task that seemed too big for me became one of the greatest blessings of my young life. There were so many life lessons that were permanently imprinted into my heart through the adversity of that first summer.

- I learned hard work.
- I learned some mechanics and maintenance skills.
- I learned that the job isn't done until the boss is happy.

- I learned the value of a dollar.
- I learned the proud feeling of a job well-done.

It was difficult, but in the end I was so glad that my dad had accepted that summer job for me. When all was said and done, I realized that it was worth it. That job was in my best interest after all.

Can you look at the pain and agony of your life and see how it has been for your good? Do you see how it has made you stronger? Do you see how it has brought you closer to God? The Bible promises that all things work together for good to them who love God. *"And we know that all things work together for good to them that love God, to them who are the called according to his purpose."* (Romans 8:28) That's a Biblical promise that is not up for debate. It's just true. Whatever trial or difficulty that you have endured was meant and designed for your betterment.

Throughout the Bible, we see time and time again how God used a tragic situation or unfortunate set of circumstances to accomplish great good. The great Apostle Paul recognized this truth when he viewed the affliction that he had to endure. *"But I would ye should understand, brethren, that the things which happened unto me have fallen out rather unto the furtherance of the gospel."* (Philippians 1:12) Paul understood that everything that had happened to him had accomplished an amazing work—specifically the spreading of the Gospel.

Look at the pain and suffering that you have experienced in your life. What has it done for you? Has it brought you closer to God? We have already seen that one of the number-one reasons why God gives us trials and tribulations is to draw us to Him. *"I will go and return to my place, till they acknowledge their offence, and seek my face: in their affliction they will seek me early."* (Hosea 5:15)

Has affliction improved your prayer life? The Word of God exhorts those that are burdened to seek God through prayer. *"Is any among you afflicted? let him pray."* (James 5:13a) Has affliction strengthened you and prepared you for something bigger than yourself? Think about David from the Bible for a moment. When he killed Goliath, that was quite a victory—but it wasn't unprecedented for David. God had already prepared him physically to fight something bigger than he should have been able to defeat. He had already been tested in that arena and had been provided with the strength and resolve to handle Goliath.

> "*And David said unto Saul, Thy servant kept his father's sheep, and there came a lion, and a bear, and took a lamb out of the flock:* ³⁵*And I went out after him, and smote him, and delivered it out of his mouth: and when he arose against me, I caught him by his beard, and smote him, and slew him.* ³⁶*Thy servant slew both the lion and the bear: and this uncircumcised Philistine shall be as one of them, seeing he hath defied the armies of the living God.* ³⁷*David said moreover, The LORD that delivered me out of the paw of the lion, and out of the paw of the bear, he will deliver me out of the hand of this Philistine.* ³⁸*And Saul said unto David, Go, and the LORD be with thee.*" (I Samuel 17:34-37)

It didn't hurt David that he had already fought a few battles in his life when he was about to go into the largest fight of his life to that point. Maybe God has brought you through a few struggles as well because He knows that you are going to defeat a giant and win the war one day. But you'll never be prepared and ready to face your Goliath until you've conquered the lions and bears.

We learn so much about life and about God through the difficulties that we experience, don't we? We learn what manner of Man God truly is. We see His power and His comfort. We experience firsthand the meaning of having a Friend Who is closer than a brother. We learn about His truths. The great prince of preachers, Charles Spurgeon, once accurately observed, "Most of the grand truths of God have to be learned by trouble; they must be burned into us by the hot iron of affliction. Otherwise, we shall not truly receive them." The "hot iron of affliction" is often the only way that we can discover the amazing and infinite nature of our Saviour and Creator.

When I take a step back and look at my own life, I indeed see how everything that I have experienced (and some would say endured) has truly been for my good. I wouldn't and couldn't be the person that I am now without each and every painful, yet wonderful step that God has ordained for my life. Am I a perfect person? That's kind of a funny thought actually. Of course I'm not. Actually, I'm not even close—not even re-motely close. But I know that God has already taught me tremendous lessons, and I can't wait to see what else He has in store. I am so thankful for the tumors, arthritis, medication, trips to the doctor, and everything else that has been such a large part of my entire life thus far because with-out all of that I would not be…well, me. I don't want to even think about what kind of a person I might be right now without all of experiences that I've gone through in the last 18 years. I'd be a completely different person…but I don't think a better person. The physical problems that I have endured can only last for a short time. One day I will pass away from this earth, and the physical problems of this life will be gone forever. However, the truths and lessons that have been burned into my heart through my medical situations will truly have eternal ramifications. *"For our light affliction, which is but for a moment, worketh for us a far more exceeding and eternal weight of glory."* (II Corinthians 4:17)

It is a certainty that God will give us the strength to endure whatever it is that we must experience while we are here on earth. But with Him by our side, what is there to fear? What is there to resent? Why not just embrace the hardships and heartaches as gifts from a loving Father who wants to take us places that we cannot go by ourselves? He's right there beside us all the way. *"We are troubled on every side, yet not distressed; we are perplexed, but not in despair; Persecuted, but not forsaken; cast down, but not destroyed."* (II Corinthians 4:8, 9) What a powerful verse! How inspirational are those words! Troubled…but not distressed. Per-plexed…but not in despair. Forsaken and cast down…but not destroyed!

When I look at everything that God has done for me and everything that I know He has planned for me in the future, it is hard not to become overwhelmed with the wonderful goodness of Christ. My heart over-flows with thankfulness and gratitude to God for the hardships that He has brought into my life! I speak truthfully as Paul did in II Corinthians 12:10 when he said, *"Therefore I take pleasure in infirmities, in re-proaches, in necessities, in persecutions, in distresses for Christ's sake: for when I am weak, then am I strong."* That verse is so blissfully true! When I am weak…then am I truly strong! When I can't take another step…

that's when God finally has the opportunity to show His power and love in an awesome way.

Of course I never knew her personally, but when I think about someone who was truly and severely afflicted by God, my mind instantly rests upon Helen Keller. I cannot even begin to comprehend the level of physical, mental, and emotional stress that this dear person experienced during her life. We consider being deaf to be quite a disadvantage. Being blind is also deemed a serious handicap. To be both blind and deaf is somewhat inconceivable. Think for a moment about just the pure isolation of such a condition. She never heard a human voice. It would have been very difficult to be fully aware of her surroundings. Consider how often she must have been frightened or scared of the unknown. Maybe she wasn't, but I would have been. The darkness would have been impenetrable. The silence must have been excruciating. From a human perspective, Helen Keller was truly a lady who suffered.

But most everyone knows enough about Helen Keller to know that she never allowed her perceived handicaps to limit her. She accomplished great things during her life and made tremendous strides through perseverance and determination. No doubt she reached heights that no one would have ever considered possible considering her physical limitations. Why was she able to overcome all of the obstacles in her way? I believe it boils down not only to the strength and grace that she must have received from God but also from her own personal attitude toward her deafness and blindness. She once said, "I thank God for my handicaps; for through them, I have found myself, my work, and my God." Helen Keller understood that, through her handicaps, she had gained so much. She had been blessed in a myriad of ways. Instead of rejecting, loathing, or hating her handicaps, she was thankful for them. Through them she knew she had found who she was as a person. She had discovered the calling upon her life. And most importantly, she had been drawn closer and nearer to her great God.

That's the testimony of my life as well. The difficulties that God has brought my way have made me into the person who I am today. My physical challenges have helped me uncover significant portions of the will of God for my life. But most of all, the pain, the tears, and the vulnerability have driven me deep into the arms of One Who loves and cares for me uniquely and devotedly. I thank God for that. Not a day goes by that I do not echo the Psalmist David when he wrote, *"It is good for me that I have been afflicted; that I might learn thy statutes."* (Psalm 119:71)

Can you be thankful for the suffering that you've endured? Can you genuinely and truthfully declare that it is good for you that you have been afflicted? Do you recognize the blessings? Do you see the loving Father Who purposely designed your life with great wisdom and understanding? I hope and pray that you do. If you've never done it before, I would encourage you right now to take a minute and thank God for the "cup" that He has given you. Thank Him for it now...embrace it forever...love it with a passion!

"Out of difficulties grow miracles."

– Jean de la Bruyere

CHAPTER NINE

NOT MY WILL

Surrendering to God's Purpose

As you have read this book, you have gotten to know me somewhat. You have seen inside my world, and you have learned a little bit about the experiences that have shaped my young life. But instead of getting to know me, what I really wish is that you could somehow get to know my three absolutely amazing siblings. They indeed are the "McCroskey kids" from whom you could learn the most and whom you would enjoy being around.

First the oldest child in our house, Angela, is a wonderful young lady who I am pretty sure was born way more mature and responsible than I will ever be. Then Kimberly is nothing but a constant reminder of how much fun life really should be. She's bursting with excitement and energy at all times with a smile that electrifies a room. And my buddy Joshua is my younger brother who continually makes me realize that I am not nearly as intelligent as what I would sometimes like to think that I am. First of all, he's the perfect roommate. He is always accommodating and the most non-confrontational person I've ever known. But really, Josh is just the smartest kid I know. There are times that he says things that are so brilliant that they completely go over my head. I just stare at him while I attempt to comprehend the genius who is my brother.

One of the many ways that Josh demonstrates his sheer natural brilliance comes in the area of LEGOS. The kid could get an engineering scholarship to Harvard if he wanted. I mean, right now at 12 years old, he possesses one of the brightest and most analytical minds that I know. I am constantly and continually amazed by the construction that Joshua undertakes in the middle of our bedroom. Now the truth is that I hate LEGOS. No, really I do. I hate LEGOS for two main reasons. First of all, I couldn't build something to save my life. I have never been gifted with any form of natural mechanical or construction talent at all. In fact, I think that Josh's LEGOS are allergic to me. Literally, I can breathe in the presence of one of his architectural masterpieces, and it will fall apart. I couldn't possibly begin to enumerate the number of LEGO projects that I have single-hand-edly dismantled just by a touch...or a look. Every time I see Joshua complete another modern marvel of construction genius, I am further reminded of how inadequate of a guy I happen to be. It's sad really.

Secondly, LEGOS seem to have somewhat of a vitriolic agenda against me. I'm really not entirely sure what I did to deserve the hatred that these thousands of inanimate objects direct toward my existence, but trust me, they do everything that they possibly can to make my life as miserable as possible. Have you ever stepped on a LEGO? Yeah, I think I would rather get run over by a truck! But see, I step on LEGOS on basically a daily basis. I can walk into my bedroom, and Josh's LEGOS will actually move themselves into my path so that I will step on them and then cringe in the pain with which I am all too familiar.

What amazes me about Josh and his LEGOS is that there seems to be absolutely no end to his creativity and ingenuity. My little brother has built structures that would put the Romans and Grecians to shame. I walk into our bedroom at times and just stare in mystification at what he has just finished building. Josh is always pushing the limits and trying something new when it comes to his designs. He owns thousands of LEGOS and is seemingly able to use them all at once to construct some-thing of utter brilliance. But stop for a moment and think about the last sentence. Joshua uses his LEGOS. Well, of course he does, right? Think about it for a moment though. All of the LEGOS that Joshua has were either given to him or directly purchased by him.

So the first thing we see is that at one point or another he accepted the LEGOS. And because Josh is so great at building things and has such an architectural mind, he immediately loved his LEGOS. He embraced them as his own. But if all he ever did was accept and embrace his LEGOS, what would be accomplished? What would be built? If he just stored all of his building materials under his bed and never brought them out to build with, then he would never get to see the finished product of a beautiful and magnificent masterpiece, would he? Of course not. Nothing can really be accomplished until Joshua decides to use what he has already accepted and embraced. He has to take one more step after accepting and embracing. So do you.

One Last Step

So here we are. Hopefully at this point you have reached the place where you have accepted and dealt with the facts of your life—whatever they may be. Furthermore, I pray that you have decided that you are going to embrace and love the challenges, weaknesses, and difficulties that God has lovingly and wisely placed in your life. But there is one more step that every Christian must take if he is going to truly fulfill the purpose and plans that God has designed for him.

I have good news for you, though! This final step is most decidedly the easiest part of this entire process. If you have accepted and embraced the difficulties that God has given you, then you are probably ready for just about anything at this point. Hopefully, you are so excited about the many blessings that your Father has placed within your life that you are brimming with enthusiasm for what else God might have designed for your life.

Now here is the not-so-happy news. The next step that you have to take is possibly the most scary. Yes, this step is easy, but very few people ever take it because they are paralyzed by their own fear. The first two steps that you took were mainly introspective. They were decisions that you had to make. You had to emotionally and spiritually determine to accept and embrace the trials of your life. But with both of those steps, you didn't actually have to tangibly do anything which made things a little bit more comfortable for you. It's always nice when you can do everything that I'm suggesting without ever getting out of your recliner, isn't it?

Well, that's done now. I want to challenge you to actually take action. You have been given a gift from God, and now I believe it is time that you start using that gift if you haven't already. *"Neglect not the gift that is in thee, which was given thee by prophecy, with the laying on of the hands of the presbytery."* (I Timothy 4:14) Many causes in the world need your help and your experience. A multitude of people need your arm around their shoulder and the encouraging words that perhaps only you can give. There are things to be done and lives to be changed.

The next two chapters will contain specific acts that you can do in order to use your difficulty for the glory of God, but for now we have to make sure that you are ready to execute those actions. You have to be sure that you have reached a point of complete and total surrender. If you have been a Christian for any length of time, surrendering is probably a theme that you have heard taught and preached on many times. But throughout this chapter, I want to show how surrendering to the will of God is critical to using your "cup" for the glory of God—even when you may not know what the will of God might be. This chapter demands honesty, and you and I will have to be brutally direct about the consequences of refusing to surrender to the purpose and plan of God. We will have to take a close look at our lives and how much control we really have allowed God to have over our words and deeds. Whether we are terrified or whether we are enthusiastic…we have to surrender.

Surrendering Requires Rejecting Fear

I hate heights. That's the simple truth—no caveats, no exceptions, and certainly no chance of that fact ever changing. I hate heights, and that's the end of it. Just recently, I recounted to my mom a story surrounding my lack of appreciation for high places.

I was attending an event at a city park which had a monument that you could go to the top of. You got inside of a little elevator and zipped straight up into the night's air. I was at the event with a friend of mine, and after a little while, it seemed like practically everybody there had gone to the top of the monument and soaked in the view of the park except for my friend and me. Now of course because of my natural fear of heights, I had no intention of ever stepping foot into that elevator. However, I started to worry about how my friend was perceiving my seeming a lack of interest in visiting the monument. My friend wasn't going to think that I was scared, right? Well, I couldn't risk it. I had to go to the top of the tower just to make sure that everyone knew I could handle it. So we squeezed into the elevator and began the steep climb to the top. When we got out of the elevator, I began to fully realize what a miserable mistake I had committed. Once we stepped out of the elevator, we found ourselves standing on a floor that had holes in it! We could literally look down at our feet and see the tiny people underneath us. That was not a pleasant feeling. Suddenly I was feeling dizzy and just a little bit sick to my stomach. I think we were at the top of the tower for all of about 30 seconds before I casually recommended that we should go back down. To my extreme relief, my friend readily agreed.

What I found out weeks later was that my friend happened to be every bit as afraid of heights as I was! Neither one of us wanted to go to the top of that tower, yet we both did. Why? We gave in to a fear. We both gave in to the fear of being embarrassed in front of the other person. And perhaps the irony of the situation is that we both allowed one fear to control another. We let our fear of humiliation dominate our fear of heights. What struck me about this entire situation was how many decisions people make based solely on the basis of what they fear. How many people allow their life to be dictated by what scares them? How many people never do what they are supposed to simply because they are afraid? What never happens because we're all too gripped by fear? Now that's a scary thought.

Here is what you need to know about fear. It's wrong. It's unbiblical. It's sinful. It doesn't come from God. A little bit blunt, right? II Timothy 1:6-9 bluntly says,

> *"Wherefore I put thee in remembrance that thou stir up the gift of God, which is in thee by the putting on of my hands. ⁷For God hath not given us the spirit of fear; but of power, and of love, and of a sound mind. ⁸Be not thou therefore ashamed of the testimony of our Lord, nor of me his prisoner: but be thou partaker of the afflictions of the gospel according to the power of God; ⁹Who hath saved us, and called us with an holy calling, not according to our own works, but according to his own purpose and grace, which was given us in Christ Jesus before the world began."*

We see first of all the call to *"stir up the gift of God, which is in thee."* What does that mean? It means to use what God has given to us for the glory of the Father. Secondly, we see that *"God hath not given us the spirit of fear."* This whole idea of immobility is nothing more than a ploy of Satan intended to make us unproductive Christian servants. And then finally we see the clear doctrine that God has called us with a purpose in mind. Again, there is a reason for the suffering that we endure in this life, but it is all for naught if we are so crippled by fear that we never fulfill the purpose of God. Never surrendering to the plan and purpose of God due to fear is one of the worst mistakes a Christian can make. God's design for a Christian's life is not something to be feared. Indeed, it is the thought of not accomplishing the will of God for my life that scares me! Never let fear make your decisions for you. We must rise above the natural inhibitions that vie for power over our lives. Go ahead, get to the top of the tower, and enjoy the view!

Surrendering Requires Being Unselfish

Again, I know that this sounds so direct and blunt that it can be painful, but I am merely trying to convey how serious this issue of surrender truly is. Whether or not we surrender to the will of God for our life is so important that we must talk pointedly and unashamedly about the potential emotions such as fear and selfishness that could keep us from living out the purposes of Christ. Selfishness is perhaps the most basic roadblock that we find along the path of surrender. We get so focused on ourselves and our pain that we refuse to think about the suffering of others and how we can help them. This philosophy is contradictory to what is clearly taught in the Word of God. Philippians 2:4 says, *"Look not every man on his own things, but every man also on the things of others."* It's not about us. At least, it shouldn't be about us.

Until we reach a point where we are willing to lose everything for the sake of Christ and others, then it will be difficult for God to use us at all. Paul reached this point when he said, *"Yea doubtless, and I count all things but loss for the excellency of the knowledge of Christ Jesus my Lord: for whom I have suffered the loss of all things, and do count them but dung, that I may win Christ."* (Philippians 3:8) Paul lost everything, but he didn't care. He had won Christ and helped a multitude of people along the way. What he had suffered and endured didn't matter anymore. He was selfless and only interested in how God could use his life to glorify and bring honor to his Heavenly Father. That's the point we have to reach as well.

Refusing to Surrender Is Rebellion

It's official. We've now abandoned all tact, and the gauntlet has been thrown down. This gets directly to the heart of the issue. Refusing to surrender to whatever God would have us to do with our life and specifically with our difficulties and weaknesses is nothing short of pure rebellion against Him. The bottom line is that God has done so much for us, yet many are so unwilling to do anything in return for Him. And when a Christian rebels against God, he literally constructs a barrier between himself and Christ, a barrier that was supposed to have been broken down a long time ago.

Before we were saved, there was a wall that separated us from God. But Christ broke down the wall and reconciled us to our Creator through His sacrificial death on the Cross.

> *"But now in Christ Jesus ye who sometimes were far off are made nigh by the blood of Christ.* [14]*For he is our peace, who hath made both one, and hath broken down the middle wall of partition between us;* [15]*Having abolished in his flesh the enmity, even the law of commandments contained in ordinances; for to make in himself of twain one new man, so making peace."* (Ephesians 2:13-15)

And what is our response to that? We build the wall right back up again by rebelling.

If you've never surrendered to God's will and His purpose for your life, it is because at some level you are harboring rebellion in your soul. I encourage you to let it go. I promise you that surrendering to God is worth stepping out by faith and letting Him do with your life what He has planned. Remember what we talked about earlier? That part about God's loving you? That's still true. And therefore it is safe to assume that if we give in and allow God to have control over how He uses us, He is going to make sure that we are okay. He's going to take care of us. He loves us. He wants us to be happy. And trust me, surrendering to God and allowing Him to use our difficulties for His glory will make us happy. But we'll talk more about that subject later in another chapter. For now, we simply have to make the conscious decision to let God in, to allow Him to have control over our lives, to consecrate our pain and suffering to Him, and to tell Him that He is free to use our adversity however He sees fit. From there, it will get a whole lot easier. I promise.

Surrender Is Reasonable

Not long ago I became very upset with myself. I'm not entirely sure why I was in such a retrospective mood, but I began to think back to all of the many things that my parents had told me to do growing up that I had complained or made a big deal about. As I look back on the tasks that my parents told me to do about which I got so upset, I turn red with embarrassment.

- Was taking out the trash really such a big deal?
- Is doing the dishes (even if it is a girl's job) actually worth getting all worked up about?

It's pretty silly some of the stuff that makes us so upset sometimes, isn't it? My parents never asked me to find a cure for cancer, solve world hunger, or negotiate world peace. They just wanted me to do a few chores. And especially when you consider everything that my parents had done for me in life, they had asked a reasonable service of me.

When God asks for us to surrender to His perfect purpose and plan, He is also simply asking for a reasonable service. *"I beseech you therefore, brethren, by the mercies of God, that ye present your bodies a living sacrifice, holy, acceptable unto God, which is your reasonable service."* (Romans 12:1) It's not that big of a deal. It's really not. In light of the unbelievable blessings and mercies that He daily bestows upon us, it is quite reasonable for us to allow Him to use us as He will. As God reveals to you how He would like to use your difficulties or trials for His honor and glory, keep in mind that it is your reasonable service. You can do it. I know you can.

We Must Surrender in Order to Help Others

If there is one topic that we have covered extensively in this book, it is the fact that God absolutely has a reason and purpose for everything that He allows into our life. He wants us to grow, learn, or be strengthened. But for this section of the book, it is critical that we look past ourselves and what we can gain personally from our afflictions. Now it's time to transition and see how perhaps our pain and tribulations can help other people around us as well. This is really the final step that has to be taken in order to truly maximize the benefits that can be gleaned from what we consider the negative circumstances of life. Accepting and embracing our difficulties mainly deals with us. How are we going to react to the painful situations? But when we start talking about using our difficulties, we are mostly talking about how we can use our suffering to benefit others. How can God take our weakness and turn it into the inspiration, comfort, and encouragement that someone else so desperately needs?

The book of Esther contains a perfect illustration of someone who surrendered in order to help those who needed her. Esther was the queen of Persia during a time when the Jewish people had been sentenced to a massacre by decree of the king. The only chance for the Jewish people's survival rested in whether or not Queen Esther could persuade the king of Persia to reverse the proclamation that he had decreed concerning the fate of the Jews. The problem for Esther was that she would have to risk her life in the effort to help the Jews. If she went to see the king without being invited by him, she risked immediate death. But Esther's uncle Mordecai convinced her to go to the king by pointing out a very significant truth.

> *"For if thou altogether holdest thy peace at this time, then shall there enlargement and deliverance arise to the Jews from another place; but thou and thy father's house shall be destroyed: and who knoweth whether thou art come to the kingdom for such a time as this?* [15]*Then Esther bade them return Mordecai this answer,* [16]*Go, gather together all the Jews that are present in Shushan, and fast ye for me, and neither eat nor drink three days, night or day: I also*

and my maidens will fast likewise; and so will I go in unto the king, which is not according to the law: and if I perish, I perish."

(Esther 4:14-16)

Mordecai asked a simple question: *"...and who knoweth whether thou art come to the kingdom for such a time as this?"* He realized that God had placed Esther in a very powerful position for the purpose of rescuing the Jewish people. What Esther had to do was recognize her opportunity and take advantage of her position. And of course we see from the Bible that she did just that. Esther surrendered by saying, *"...if I perish, I perish."* Her words revealed her resolution, her willingness to sacrifice, and her surrender.

Here is what we have to recognize as well. We have an opportunity to take advantage of our position, situation, and experience. There are people whom we can help as well. There are lives that we can touch. There are friends whom we can influence. There are broken hearts and lives that we can help piece back together. Just like Esther, we have a unique chance to help those around us. God has placed in our lives the difficulties and therefore the opportunities that we need in order to make a difference in our world.

But what's the first step? The first step is surrender. Just like Queen Esther, we have to look heavenward and decide that we will leave what happens up to God, but we will do what we know is right. And if we perish…we perish. But we've won the first battle already. We've surrendered.

God Will Not Call Us to Do Something That He Has Not Equipped Us to Handle

Are you scared yet? That whole *"...if I perish, I perish"* thing is a little bit intimidating, isn't it? Actually, just the thought of God's wanting us to do something at all can be a little bit scary. Probably Esther had a few moments where she wondered, "When did I sign up to be responsible for saving a nation?" Maybe you're wondering what God is going to ask you to do. Perhaps you're worried. "What if He wants me to do to something big? What if it is bigger than me? What if I cannot handle it?" So many questions to be answered, right?

Well, here is the answer: don't worry about it! I'm serious. Just stop thinking about it. Why? Because one simple truth covers all of the endless questions that may be circulating through your mind. God will not call you to do something that He has not already equipped you to handle. It's that simple. Allow me to show two examples in the Bible of how God uses weakness to become strength for others.

"And there came an angel of the LORD, and sat under an oak which was in Ophrah, that pertained unto Joash the Abiezerite: and his son Gideon threshed wheat by the winepress, to hide it from the Midianites. ¹²And the angel of the LORD appeared unto him, and said unto him, The LORD is with thee, thou mighty man of valour. ¹³And Gideon said unto him, Oh my Lord, if the LORD be with us, why then is all this befallen us? And where be all his miracles which our fathers told us of, saying, Did not the LORD bring us up from Egypt? But now the LORD hath forsaken us, and delivered us unto the hands of the Midianites. ¹⁴And the LORD looked upon him, and said, Go in this thy might, and thou shalt save Israel from the hand of the Midianites: have not I sent thee? ¹⁵And he said, Oh my Lord, wherewith shall I save Israel? behold, my family is poor in Manasseh, and I am the least of my father's house. ¹⁶And the LORD said unto him, Surely I will be with thee, and thou shalt smite the Midianites as one man." (Judges 6:11-16)

The angel of the Lord came to Gideon and informed him that God wanted him to defeat the Midianites. What was Gideon's immediate reaction? Trepidation! Gideon instantly started trying to remind God that he was a poor man from a poor family, and he couldn't possibly be a good choice to deliver the Israelite people. God's counter reply was quite simple yet incredibly profound: *"...have not I sent thee?"* The implication surely seems to be that Gideon is capable of anything because God would not have sent him in the first place unless He knew that Gideon was already prepared and equipped for the task at hand.

God has prepared you for a task as well. Your immediate reaction might be that you can't do it, but you have to realize that God wouldn't be asking you to do something unless He was sure that you were able to execute the orders you have been given. Another example of this truth can be found in the book of Jeremiah.

> *"Then the word of the LORD came unto me, saying, ⁵Before I formed thee in the belly I knew thee; and before thou camest forth out of the womb I sanctified thee, and I ordained thee a prophet unto the nations. ⁶Then said I, Ah, Lord GOD! behold, I cannot speak: for I am a child. ⁷But the LORD said unto me, Say not, I am a child: for thou shalt go to all that I shall send thee, and whatsoever I command thee thou shalt speak. ⁸Be not afraid of their faces: for I am with thee to deliver thee, saith the LORD. ⁹Then the LORD put forth his hand, and touched my mouth. And the LORD said unto me, Behold, I have put my words in thy mouth. ¹⁰See, I have this day set thee over the nations and over the kingdoms, to root out, and to pull down, and to destroy, and to throw down, to build, and to plant."* (Jeremiah 1:4-10)

God called Jeremiah for a preordained purpose, but Jeremiah had a natural resistance to surrendering to God's plans. Jeremiah makes a very basic and simplistic excuse; he thinks he cannot speak well. But God again takes away this excuse by reminding Jeremiah that He has already prepared him to be a prophet to the nations. God had created Jeremiah for the specific reason of being a prophet, and He told Jeremiah that He would provide him with all of the tools to be a prophet that he needed. God would give him the words to say and direct him in how to articulate them. God obviously had a purpose in mind for Jeremiah's life. *"See, I have this day set thee over the nations and over the kingdoms, to root out, and to pull down, and to destroy, and to throw down, to build, and to plant."*

Just like He had a plan for Jeremiah, God has a purpose for your life as well. You might be scared. You might not think you are ready. You might think God has made a mistake. But please realize that He has called you to a task that He has already prepared you to accomplish. How has He prepared you? All of the trials, difficulties, and painful experiences through which you have suffered have molded you into the person that God needs in order to accomplish His will for your life.

Now the decision rests in your hands. You can use the difficulties that God has given you and surrender to the purpose and plan for your life…or you can run.

Do Not Run From God's Purpose

Probably the most universal example of someone's running from God instead of surrendering to His will is found through the exploration of the life of Jonah.

> *"Now the word of the LORD came unto Jonah the son of Amittai, saying, [2]Arise, go to Ninevah, that great city, and cry against it; for their wickedness is come up before me. [3]But Jonah rose up to flee unto Tarshish from the presence of the LORD, and went down to Joppa; and he found a ship going to Tarshish: so he paid the fare thereof, and went down into it, to go with them to Tarshish from the presence of the LORD."* (Jonah 1:1-3)

God had a purpose for the life of Jonah, but he was unwilling to submit himself to that plan.

Now of course it's one thing to make a concrete statement such as "Do not run from God's purpose," but it's quite another thing when you consider the consequences of refusing to surrender to the will of God. *"Then Jonah prayed unto the LORD his God out of the fish's belly, And said, I cried by reason of mine affliction unto the LORD, and he heard me; out of the belly of hell cried I, and thou heardest my voice."* (Jonah 2:1, 2) The Bible says that out of the belly of hell Jonah cried to the Lord. Nothing good comes from running away from God. It's true. Jonah ran in the first place because he was rebelling against God's call on his life, but in the end he found himself in a far worse predicament. You really will be happier and much more satisfied after you relinquish your will and allow God to use you and your pain however He will.

The decision is yours. You can surrender to the will of God and reap the blessings of a life yielded to Christ, or you can buy a ticket and set sail for Tarshish…and probably end up in your own personal belly of Hell. Am I trying to scare you into surrendering to God? No! I am just trying to be honest. I feel like writing this book was God's calling me to start using my experiences and pain to try to help other people.

I had two options: write the book and allow God to use it however He will or refuse to act upon the clear call of God in my life. I know beyond a shadow of a doubt that if I would have chosen the latter, there would be no way that I could be as happy as what I am right now in life. I know that right now at this moment as I write this chapter, I am working on accomplishing His plan for my life. If I refused to surrender and write this book, I would not have that security or that peace. Don't run from the call of God. He has a purpose and a plan for you. You may not even know what that design is yet, but that's not important. What's important is that you surrender right now to whatever it is God wants you to do.

> *"See then that ye walk circumspectly, not as fools, but as wise,* [16]*Redeeming the time, because the days are evil.* [17]*Wherefore be ye not unwise, but understanding what the will of the Lord is."*
>
> (Ephesians 5:15-17)

God Can Compensate for Our Weakness

In Exodus we find the story of God's calling the great leader of Israel, Moses, to guide the oppressed children of Israel out of the captivity of the Egyptians.

> *"And the angel of the* LORD *appeared unto him in a flame of fire out of the midst of a bush: and he looked, and, behold, the bush burned with fire, and the bush was not consumed.* [3]*And Moses said, I will now turn aside, and see this great sight, why the bush is not burnt.* [4]*And when the* LORD *saw that he turned aside to see, God called unto him out of the midst of the bush, and said, Moses, Moses.* [5]*And he said, Here am I. And he said, Draw not nigh hither: put off thy shoes from off thy feet, for the place whereon thou standest is holy ground.* [6]*Moreover he said, I am the God of thy father, the God of Abraham, the God of Isaac, and the God of Jacob. And Moses hid his face; for he was afraid to look upon God.* [7]*And the* LORD *said, I have surely seen the affliction of my people which are in Egypt, and have heard their cry by reason of their taskmasters; for I know their sorrows;* [8]*And I am come down to*

deliver them out of the hand of the Egyptians, and to bring them up out of that land unto a good land and a large, unto a land flowing with milk and honey; unto the place of the Canaanites, and the Hittites, and the Amorites, and the Perizzites, and the Hivites, and the Jebusites. ⁹Now therefore, behold, the cry of the children of Israel is come unto me: and I have also seen the oppression wherewith the Egyptians oppress them. ¹⁰Come now therefore, and I will send thee unto Pharaoh, that thou mayest bring forth my people the children of Israel out of Egypt." (Exodus 3:2-10)

This passage reveals how the people of Israel were brutally afflicted by the Egyptians. God had decided in His wisdom that now was the time to release His people from their imprisonment and lead them to the Promised Land that He had prepared for them. But look at what God does. He chose to use a human instrument to help those who were afflicted. Part of God's design for Moses' life was to be used to help others who were suffering. Perhaps that is part of God's plan for your life as well. But instead of embracing the call of God upon his life, Moses began to make excuses for why he could not be used in this area.

"And Moses said unto God, Who am I, that I should go unto Pharaoh, and that I should bring forth the children of Israel out of Egypt? And he said, Certainly I will be with thee; and this shall be a token unto thee, that I have sent thee: When thou hast brought forth the people of Egypt, ye shall serve God upon this mountain." (Exodus 3:11, 12)

The first excuse: Moses says that he doesn't have the clout or credentials to do something so great.

God's reply: I have sent you. I will be with you. You will be successful.

"And Moses said unto God, Behold, when I come unto the children of Israel, and shall say unto them, The God of your fathers hath sent me unto you; and they shall say to me, What is his name? what shall I say unto them? And God said unto Moses, I AM THAT I AM: and he said, Thus shalt thou say unto the children of Israel, I AM hath sent me unto you." (Exodus 3:13, 14)

The second excuse: Moses says that he doesn't know what to tell the people when they ask him who sent him.

God's response: Tell them the God of your fathers has sent you. Tell them I AM has sent you.

"And Moses answered and said, But, behold, they will not believe me, nor hearken unto my voice: for they will say, The LORD hath not appeared unto thee. ²And the LORD said unto him, What is that in thine hand? And he said, A rod. ³And he said, Cast it on the ground. And he cast it on the ground, and it became a serpent; and Moses fled from before it. ⁴And the LORD said unto Moses, Put forth thine hand, and take it by the tail. And he put forth his hand, and caught it, and it became a rod in his hand: ⁵That they may believe that the LORD God of their fathers, the God of Abraham, the God of Isaac, and the God of Jacob, hath appeared unto thee." (Exodus 4:1-5)

The third excuse: Moses says the Israelites will not believe him.

God's response: He gives Moses a series of miracles that he can perform in order to prove his call to the children of Israel.

"And Moses said unto the LORD, O my LORD, I am not eloquent, neither heretofore, nor since thou hast spoken unto thy servant: but I am slow of speech, and of a slow tongue. ¹¹And the LORD said unto him, Who hath made man's mouth? or who maketh the dumb, or deaf, or the seeing, or the blind? Have not I the LORD? ¹²Now therefore go, and I will be with thy mouth, and teach thee what thou shalt say. ¹³And he said, O my Lord, send, I pray thee, by the hand of him whom thou wilt send. ¹⁴And the anger of the LORD was kindled against Moses, and he said, Is not Aaron the Levite thy brother? I know that he can speak well. And also, behold, he cometh forth to meet thee: and when he seeth thee, he will be glad in his heart. ¹⁵And thou shalt speak unto him, and put words in his mouth: and I will be with thy mouth, and with his mouth, and will teach you what ye shall do. ¹⁶And he shall be thy spokesman unto the people: and he shall be, even he shall be to thee instead of a mouth, and thou shalt be to him instead of God. And thou shalt take this rod in thine hand, wherewith thou shalt do signs." (Exodus 4:10-16)

The fourth excuse: Moses says that he cannot speak well and will not be able to effectively or persuasively communicate with the Israelites.

God's response: I will provide you with an eloquent spokesman who already knows you well.

Are you starting to catch the theme? God is in the business of stripping away excuses and compensating for weaknesses. I have a theory on this story of Moses' call to leadership. I think the first three excuses that he offered were merely masks for the real reason why he did not think he could lead the children of Israel. The real reason why he was unwilling to immediately surrender to the call of God was that he was insecure regarding his weakness or challenge in life: the fact that he wasn't an articulate speaker. Moses did not think that he could be used by God effectively because of this difficulty that he possessed. But what he did not know was that God wanted to use the fact that he could not speak well to bring even more honor and glory to Himself.

God wanted to make a great leader out of a man who was not a great orator or master public speaker. God wanted to use a person who was afflicted to help other people who were suffering as well. That's what He wants to do with us, too. But do you know what we have to do? The same thing that Moses did. Surrender! Eventually Moses surrendered to the call of God and wrought a great work through the power of God. We can do the same thing. God can compensate for our weaknesses and difficulties as well. We just have to let him. *"Now unto him that is able to do exceeding abundantly above all that we ask or think, according to the power that worketh in us."* (Ephesians 3:20)

Surrender Is Worth the Reward

*"And he came out, and went, as he was wont, to the mount of Olives; and his disciples also followed him. [40]And when he was at the place, he said unto them, Pray that ye enter not into temptation. [41]And he was withdrawn from them about a stone's cast, and kneeled down, and prayed, [42]Saying, Father, if thou be willing, remove this cup from me: nevertheless **not my will**, but thine, be done. [43]And there appeared an angel unto him from heaven,*

strengthening him. [44]*And being in an agony he prayed more earnestly: and his sweat was as it were great drops of blood falling down to the ground.* [45]*And when he rose up from prayer, and was come to his disciples, he found them sleeping for sorrow."*

(Luke 22:39-45)

Christ surrendered. He asked God to remove his cup if it was possible, but if it wasn't…that was acceptable too. He would handle it. God had equipped Him to handle it. He wasn't going to run. He wasn't going to hide. He wasn't going to be afraid. He wasn't going to be selfish. He surrendered. And what came of His surrender? Salvation for the entire world was the result. Out of great suffering came great reward. It was worth it. The pain, the agony, and the suffering that Christ endured through His sacrifice was worth it. He surrendered…thank God He did.

Have you given in? Have you surrendered? Have you let go of your fear, selfishness, and rebellion? Have you realized that surrendering to your Father is nothing more than reasonable? Do you realize that He has called you with a purpose? Do you understand that He has afflicted you with a plan in mind? Do you see how He has already equipped you to do great things for Him? Have you surrendered?

Be Strong and Courageous

I haven't promised you that it will be easy. I didn't assure you that life will always be simple and peaceful. It wasn't peaceful for Christ to hang on a cross naked and alone. But He did it anyway. Surrender requires courage. *"There shall not any man be able to stand before thee all the days of thy life: as I was with Moses, so I will be with thee: I will not fail thee, nor forsake thee. Be strong and of a good courage: for unto this people shalt thou divide for an inheritance the land, which I sware unto their fathers to give them. Only be thou strong and very courageous…."* (Joshua 1:5-7)

With God Almighty by our side, no man will be able to stand against us. But you know what we have to do in order for God to stand next to us? We first have to stand. We have to stand up and determine to use the pain and suffering that God has given to us. We have to surrender our will and allow Him to use us and our experiences as He will.

Christ looked Heavenward while He was suffering in great agony, and He said, *"...not my will, but thine, be done."* Fellow Christian, it's time we do the same.

"*Character cannot be developed
in ease and quiet.
Only through experience
of trial and suffering
can the soul be strengthened,
ambition inspired,
and success achieved.*"

– Helen Keller

CHAPTER TEN

MAKING A DIFFERENCE

Investing in Others

I very much believe that everything that I have written so far is very important; I wouldn't have spent so much time working on it if I thought it was insignificant. But I have a confession to make. We are finally at the part of the book that I have been looking forward to the most! Using our difficulty in a tangible way to help other people is what I consider the most exciting part of this entire accepting, embracing, and utilization process. This is where the fun starts. This is when we start really seeing the awesome hand of God working not just in, but through us as well.

God may have given you the cup from which you have had to drink in life for a myriad of different reasons. Maybe we have touched on these reasons already, and for some of you, reasons that only you could ever know and understand. But no matter why God chose to afflict you, one by-product of your suffering should absolutely, without a doubt, come to fruition. That result is the willingness and ability to help those around you who are also suffering—especially those who are afflicted with similar cups to yours.

Think about the people whom you know. Is there anyone you know who does not have a heartache? Is there anyone who hasn't gone through a dark time? How many of them are struggling right now? Who is helping them? Who has his arm around their shoulder? Who is drying their tears? Who is telling them that there is at least one person praying for them every night? Is it you? What are you doing to help? You've struggled too. You've been there. You've hurt. You've cried. You know what they're feeling. Are you behind them holding them up in the love of Christ? One last question: are you making a difference? That's a pretty profound question, and it is one to answer honestly.

I think the most important way that we can use the burdens and challenges that God has given us is to invest in other people. Because of what you've gone through, you have a unique experience to use in the effort to help someone else. There are so many hurting people in the world. So many people are lost and looking for encouragement and hope. You could be the source of inspiration to them. You could help them. You could make a difference. But you have to want to make a difference. You have to make a conscious effort to be there when it counts for the people around you.

Why do so few people ever take the time and make the effort to invest in someone else's life? The answer is quite simple. Investing in someone else does take time and does require effort. It's not easy. People are not always pleasant. People will use you. People will hurt you. You have to open yourself up to a point of vulnerability. You have to put yourself "out there." You have to be willing to tell your story. But then again…it's worth it.

When I first felt the nudging of God to write this book, my immediate reaction was "no." I loved to write. I've always enjoyed it. It wasn't necessarily that I was unwilling to put in the time and effort required in the writing process. I was scared of telling my story. I was afraid of what people would think. Would the readers be receptive? How would that affect my privacy? Do I really want to expose myself to anyone who picks up a copy of this book? Yeah, I wasn't so sure about that.

But then I started to think about the other side of the coin. Perhaps my story could help someone else. Maybe I could make a difference in a life. There was a chance that God wanted to use my affliction to inspire, encourage, and strengthen. I couldn't pass on that opportunity. I had to go for it. If writing a book is one way that God wanted to use me, then I could do that. It wasn't just about serving other people. It was also about serving God.

I am thankful for my physical problems because I have a unique way to serve God. Service to God is a very vital portion of a Christian's responsibility to God and the local church. Most pastors would never have trouble getting things done at the church if they could just get every one of their members to do one thing. Sunday school classes would never go without teachers. Buses would never lack drivers. The church building would never become dirty. Every new visitor would be greeted and followed up on. Visitation would be more fruitful, and more people would come to know Christ as their Saviour. All of these things would become realities if Christians took service to God seriously. It's really the least that Christians can do, you know? God saved us from Hell along with giving us the innumerable other blessings that He showers on our life. The church provides us with the opportunity to fellowship with like-minded people, sing praises to God, and hear the Word of God preached. We have received and continue to receive so much from God and the local church that Christian service really seems like a minor requirement, doesn't it?

Because we all have unique problems, we all have unique opportunities to help those around us as we serve God. The most obvious example in my life of this truth would be the writing of this book. Would I really be writing this book if I didn't have so many physical problems? Maybe, but I doubt it. Would you really be reading this book if I didn't have the medical history that I do? Maybe, but again, I doubt it. Seriously, who would read a book that was written by a person who was not an expert in that field? Would you read a book about politics written by a chef? Would you read a book about cooking written by a political analyst? Maybe you would, but I think you'd be in the minority on that one. I certainly don't imagine that I'd have the privilege of writing this book if I didn't have arthritis and live my life in continual pain. I'm having a blast writing this book though, so I'm very thankful that I have arthritis and am able to write from an experienced point of view. The writing of this book has been a thrill for me, and I truly hope that it is a blessing and an encouragement to somebody who will read it in the future. I am thankful for the unique way that God has provided a way for me to serve Him due to my physical problems.

Now maybe you are thinking to yourself, "Great, I'm happy for you, but God hasn't called me to write a book. I don't even like books. So what is a unique way that I can serve God because of my pain?" That is a very good point. God has certainly not called everyone to write a book. Sometimes I meet people that I'm not sure God has even called to read books. However, there are many other unique and different ways to serve God other than writing a book. It really depends upon the specific source that causes your pain as to how you can specifically serve God, but there are ways we can all use our pain to serve God and others.

Encourage Others

An obvious way to serve God would be to encourage and motivate others, especially those with similar issues. Most people need someone else in their life to push them and motivate them to excel. Maybe for you that's a parent, a friend, a pastor, a youth pastor, or a sibling. The majority of people, though, do not "self-motivate." Ask a parent how many toys would get picked up if they never motivated their child to clean up. Ask a youth pastor how much he gets out of his teenagers if he doesn't excite and push them to accomplish a specified goal. It may sound like the parent and the youth pastor are being hard on the children and the teenagers, but the truth is that it is in the best interest of people to have someone else encouraging them. Everybody needs somebody to whom he can look and regain perspective, encouragement, and motivation.

Having a physical problem and living with pain is a great asset if you wish to be an encouragement to other people's lives. I can't physiologically explain to you why people respect or "look up to" people who live in pain, but they do. It's just a fact. Maybe it's because people who have suffered are perceived as tough, compassionate, and resilient. Many times people will see a quality or character trait in your life that they desire for themselves. They see qualities such as faith, humility, determination, contentment, etc. Do any of those sound familiar to you? The point is, if you live in pain with a Godly attitude, you have instant credibility with most people. This credibility provides you with an excellent opportunity to encourage and motivate other people.

I personally consider it an immense privilege to impact someone's life in such a way. I hold my head a little higher and straighten my back just a little more when I even think about the possibility of inspiring, encouraging, or motivating another person. I'm certainly thankful for this opportunity. I hope that you are as well.

Maybe you have cancer. God has given you a chance to inspire others to battle through adversity. You have the opportunity to put your arm around someone who has just been diagnosed and encourage that person with your experiences. Perhaps you have chronic back pain. I know many people struggle their whole life with absolutely debilitating back pain. You never even seem to know your back is part of your body until it hurts, and then you can't stop thinking about your back! Overlooking the agony for just a moment though, you have been given a chance to encourage and motivate the countless number of others who possess the same kind of pain.

A couple of years ago, I used to go to a hospital in my town once a week to see a physical therapist. I would just go there to work on my flexibility and strength. About two years ago, my physical therapist asked me if I would be willing to talk to a 12-year-old boy who had just been diagnosed with rheumatoid arthritis. I was a little unsure of what I was supposed to say to this boy, but I agreed anyway. A couple of weeks later I met this young man. Instantly, I felt like I knew him. Now the truth is, I didn't know this guy at all. I didn't know what his interests were. I didn't know what he liked and what he didn't. I didn't even know his last name. Immediately though, I felt as if he and I had something significant in common. I had something in common with him that nobody else around him had. His parents tried to help him, but they didn't have arthritis. His doctors tried to help him, but they didn't have arthritis. His physical therapist tried to help him, but she doesn't have arthritis. I was finally someone to whom he could completely relate. Almost immediately, this 12-year-old started to open up. He told me about how he used to run cross-country events until his knees began to ache and be sore. He told me how he was having a lot of trouble writing because his wrists and fingers hurt so bad. He told me about the nausea that he had been experiencing due to a medicine that he and I were both taking at the time.

It was such an amazing blessing to me to be able to talk to that young man. I was able to encourage him, listen to him, and share with him little pain-management tricks that I had learned throughout the years. I would have never had this exhilarating opportunity if God had never given me arthritis! My opportunity to serve God and others with encouragement and motivation makes me exceedingly thankful for my arthritis and for my pain.

> *"Wherefore comfort yourselves together, and edify one another, even as also ye do. [12]And we beseech you, brethren, to know them which labour among you, and are over you in the Lord, and admonish you; [13]And to esteem them very highly in love for their work's sake. And be at peace among yourselves. [14]Now we exhort you, brethren, warn them that are unruly, comfort the feebleminded, support the weak, be patient toward all men."*
>
> (I Thessalonians 5:11-14)

Are you living out the admonishment of these verses? Who are you edifying? Who is a better, happier, more encouraged person because of your influence on him? These are tough questions, but necessary ones if we want to truly take advantage of the suffering that God has placed in our life. Make it your goal in the next year to help someone. Find someone in your church, your workplace, or your neighborhood who needs you to come along beside them and say, "Hey, I know you're going through a hard time right now, and I know a God Who can help you pull through."

Don't tell the person, "I know what you're going through." That statement really doesn't help much. Just let the person know that you are there if he needs your help. Write a note. Give the person a call. Shoot the person an email. Just let the individual know you care.

At first, he might try to shut you out. He might be in too much pain to open up. It may take a while. But persevere and don't give up until you break down the walls that he tries to put up. It's worth it. God gave you difficulties in part so that you would be able to encourage those around you during their time of affliction.

Are you edifying and encouraging someone?

Are you supporting the weak?

Are you making a difference?

Inspire Others

Several years ago I met a dear lady who lives out of state who has severe rheumatoid arthritis just like me. She is a wonderful Christian lady who could truly relate to the pain with which I deal on a daily basis. We spent quite a bit of time talking about treatments, medications, and everything that God had taught us through our common "cup." As we conversed, I was continually struck by the realization that this lady didn't let her arthritis hold her back whatsoever. Despite her literally crippling condition, she was a wife, a mother, and very involved in her church. She reinforced to me the mind-set that life wasn't over just because our joints didn't bend. She inspired me. She made a difference in my life.

So many people in my life have inspired me, and I believe they have made me a better person because of their influence. I have been truly blessed with an abundance of Godly people who have taken the time to invest in me. Probably those who have made the most significant impact on my life don't even know it! They've just always been there. They have always been a strong and solid presence that I know I can lean on when it counts.

Who are your heroes in life? Who inspires you? Is it a parent? Maybe you are inspired by a pastor, a historical figure, or just a friend. Now ask yourself why it is that this person has affected you so much. Maybe it's because the person has spent a significant amount of time investing in you. But then again, it's possible that you have never even met the person before. How is it that the individual can inspire you if you don't even personally know the person? My guess would be one of two reasons. Either you are impressed by something that the person has done, or you are impressed by something that the person has overcome.

Maybe the person has done something amazing. Maybe the person has been used to break down barriers that are not easily torn down. Perhaps the person has done the seemingly impossible. Or maybe the person has just been consistent. Perhaps the person has never done anything spectacular but has just kept doing what he was supposed to do...even when it hasn't been easy. The lady to whom I referred in this chapter as being an inspiration has not done something that has garnered her international exposure. She's never climbed Mount Everest. She's never won an Olympic gold medal. She's never raced in the Tour de France. But you know what she has done? Kept going! She has gotten out of bed when she wanted to lie there in agony. She's taken care of her family when, in truth, she needed someone to take care of her. She's lived in constant pain with a positive and Christlike spirit. That's all. But that was enough. It was enough to inspire me.

Now here is the question that you have to ask yourself: who is inspired by you? Who looks to you as a source of hope and confidence? Are you making a difference in anyone's life right now?

God has given you pain and suffering so that you can inspire those around you. But in order to do that, you have to make sure that your heart and spirit are right. These are all things that I have addressed earlier in this book. But do you see the opportunity that has been laid in front of you? You have unique experiences and insights that someone else needs. Are you using your difficulty for the glory of God and for the betterment of those around you?

Maybe you are looking around at the people in your life and thinking to yourself that there is nobody whom you can help. If that's the case, get creative. Think outside the box. Here's an example. I've never had cancer. But my parents were once told that my tumors were malignant, and thankfully, it turned out that they were always benign. So because I've never actually had cancer, does that mean that I could never help someone who does? Truthfully, I believe that assessment would be incorrect. I think I have a very unique way to encourage people with cancer, especially those going through chemotherapy.

For six years I was on a medicine named methotrexate. It is a very common arthritis medication that literally thousands of people have taken since it was released for use in juveniles. Most people tolerate this medicine fairly well. I never did—not even a little bit. When my doctor first put me on methotrexate, it was administered via injection. My mom and I would drive across town to our pediatrician's office twice a week to get the shot. After a couple of years, my mom decided to learn how to properly administer shots, and she began to give them to me at home from that point forward. As years went by, all of the possible injection sites on my body had become very tough from years of injections. As a result, the doctor recommended that my mom mix the liquid medicine into a glass of orange juice so that I could drink it. Tasty.

The administration and digestion of the drug was definitely the easy part of the process for me, however. The trouble that I ran into was how nauseated methotrexate made me feel. As soon as the medicine would interact with my system, I would begin to feel very sick. I would vomit and feel horrible for hours—sometimes days. It was practically intolerable. I would dread the time every week when I knew I had to take methotrexate. It was simply miserable. I haven't taken the drug in two years now, but to this day the very thought of it makes my stomach start feeling a little queasy. I guess at this point it's probably all physiological and nothing else, but I won't even drink orange juice anymore just because of how sick methotrexate made me. So if, for whatever reason, you ever have a doctor prescribe methotrexate…run! I'm serious. If he insists that your life depends upon it, I'd make funeral preparations. But that's just my personal suggestion.

Do you see how my experience with severe and long-time nausea would help me be able to relate or connect with a cancer patient? Thank God for that! My experience has given me a unique opportunity to inspire a large group of people while they go through the suffering that they must endure. What unique experience do you have that could be used to inspire someone else?

In Philippians 1:14, Paul remarks upon how his pain and experiences have helped to inspire other Christians. *"And many of the brethren in the Lord, waxing confident by my bonds, are much more bold to speak the word without fear."* People were more confident and bold in their speaking of the Gospel because they were inspired by that which Paul had endured. What a testimony! What a blessing for Paul to be able to look back on his life and see that he had made a difference not only in service to God, but also in the area of spurring on other Christians to greater acts of service as well. That's a testimony that I'd like to have as well. I want God to work through my life in such a spectacular way that people can look at me and be inspired to do greater things for His honor and glory. Isn't that what you want as well? If it is, you have made a great step in the direction of productively using your affliction for the benefit of others and for the service of Christ.

Comfort Others

It's probably just because I have had so many of them, but I would have to lie to tell you that surgeries even remotely bother me anymore. I don't get nervous. I don't get upset. I sleep well the night before. It's just not a big deal to me. You know that going under general anesthesia doesn't bother you when the number-one thing that upsets you about a surgery is that you can't have your daily cup of coffee in the morning! When that's your biggest concern, it's official that operations just aren't a big deal anymore.

At my last surgery, I had a sweet old man who started my IV. We were talking and laughing with each other as he prepped my hand and skillfully slipped the needle into a vein. When he was finished, he got a big smile and his face and said, "Well, that wasn't bad at all. And to think that just a month ago I was sweeping out the parking deck!" I thought it was an absolutely hilarious statement, and it actually served to further relax me as I prepared to go into the operating room. Oh, and by the way, the man had been doing IVs since before my parents were born. He definitely knew was he was doing.

The truth is, however, for many people about to go under the knife, that joke would have made them very nervous and anxious. Most people don't do well with the thought of a surgery. I know a couple of people personally who refused to have an operation at all. I was talking to a friend of mine about a month ago who told me that he had decided to deal with a permanent disability that might well be corrected with a surgery. But he is so afraid of going under anesthesia that he would rather live with the injury that he suffered a few years ago. For whatever reason, he is terrified of having an operation.

Now I can't truly relate with my friend's fear, but what I can do is try to comfort and allay the fears of the many people in his situation. In fact, the Bible commands me to do just that. Isaiah 40:1 says, *"Comfort ye, comfort ye my people, saith your God."* All of us are uniquely and specifically qualified to participate in this important area of service. The Word of God talks about how God comforts us during our suffering, in part so that we are then able to turn around and comfort those who are in need as well.

> *"Blessed be God, even the Father of our Lord Jesus Christ, the Father of mercies, and the God of all comfort; ⁴Who comforteth us in all our tribulation, that we may be able to comfort them which are in any trouble, by the comfort wherewith we ourselves are comforted of God. ⁵For as the sufferings of Christ abound in us, so our consolation also aboundeth by Christ. ⁶And whether we be afflicted, it is for your consolation and salvation, which is effectual in the enduring of the same sufferings which we also suffer: or whether we be comforted, it is for your consolation and salvation. ⁷And our hope of you is stedfast, knowing, that as ye are partakers of the sufferings, so shall ye be also of the consolation."*
>
> (II Corinthians 1:3-7)

Do you see how the pain and suffering that you have gone through has enabled and equipped you to comfort and strengthen those around you? People need your encouragement and time. In II Corinthians 7:5-7, Paul tells how God used another brother in the Lord to comfort him when he needed it most.

> *"For, when we were come into Macedonia, our flesh had no rest, but we were troubled on every side; without were fightings, within were fears. ⁶Nevertheless God, that comforteth those that are cast down, comforted us by the coming of Titus. ⁷And not by his coming only, but by the consolation wherewith he was comforted in you, when he told us your earnest desire, your mourning, your fervent mind toward me; so that I rejoiced the more."* (II Corinthians 7:5-7)

God wants to use people like Titus, you, and me to comfort those around us. That's the way that He chooses to comfort His children—by way of other Christians. In II Corinthians 7:5-7, Paul talks about having fights on the outside and fears on the inside. How many people do you know that are in that same kind of situation? Maybe you've been in that situation yourself. When I think about someone's having fights on the outside, I think specifically of physical problems. Maybe it's chronic pain, an acute illness, or a terminal disease. Has God given you a history of experiences that would allow you to minister to people such as these? He has to me.

When I think about someone's having fears on the inside, I specifically think of emotional problems. It seems like more and more people are dealing with mental and emotional issues such as depression, a lack of joy, and constant despondency. This is a much harder category of people for me to relate to because I believe God has given me an especially bright and happy outlook on life. However, I can still even in a small way relate to someone who is having a hard time digging himself out of the pit of emotional scars and wounds. There was one point in my life when I had to deal with fairly severe emotional issues.

Two summers ago I was coming off of a major reconstructive surgery on my mouth. Without top teeth to provide a natural support base, the upper palate of my mouth had slowly but surely caved in over the years. My oral surgeon and cleft palate specialist felt that it was a good time in my life to correct this issue because I had finished growing. The surgery was fairly major. The doctors had to break the bones in my jaw and quite literally move the top of my mouth into the correct position. A large plastic splint was then wired into the top of my mouth to hold the new bone structure in place as it healed. The operation itself was several hours long and quite extensive, but it was the recovery that caused me more problems than what I had anticipated.

The road to recovery was a slow and painful one for me that summer. It started with a couple of days in the hospital where I think that quite honestly all I did was bleed. I hesitate to be so blunt because I do not want to be unnecessarily gory, but I spent hours doing nothing but spitting up the blood that was ceaselessly pouring out of my mouth. Sleep was pretty much out of the question because I was in so much pain and just so uncomfortable in general. I was soon so exhausted and so weak that I began having trouble focusing on anything that could take my mind off of the surgery and all of its effects. My entire face was so swollen that I had trouble talking to anyone, and of course the huge piece of plastic wired into my mouth wasn't helping much either.

But you've probably guessed the worst part by now. What was I eating? Yeah, that wasn't too much fun. I didn't eat anything solid for over three months. Of course, I'm telling you this story because I'm giving you insight into the one time period in my life when I get did a little bit depressed. Eating through a straw for three months will do that to you. I literally would have killed a man for a slice of pizza after a couple of weeks.

At no point during that summer was I remotely suicidal, medically depressed, or even really down, but I did struggle some with feeling sorry for myself and wondering why I had to spend my summer lying on a couch eating my hundredth bowl of pea soup when most of my friends were having a great time on vacations or hanging out with each other. So in some small way I can try to relate to the increasing number of people who fight similar emotions. Maybe you've gone through a much more significant period of depression in your life. That gives you an even greater opportunity to comfort and encourage the people around you in mirroring circumstances. Are you using that opportunity?

How do you comfort someone? As we discussed earlier, it's not always the easiest thing to do. I've found the simplest two ways to offer consolation to a hurting person are to just be available for them and then to continually point them to the Father.

"Come unto me, all ye that labour and are heavy laden, and I will give you rest. 29Take my yoke upon you, and learn of me; for I am meek and lowly in heart: and ye shall find rest unto your souls. 30For my yoke is easy, and my burden is light." (Matthew 11:28-30)

He is the One Who gives the rest and heals the broken hearts. We are simply the avenue by which a person in pain can be brought to Him.

Start a Chain Reaction

Perhaps you have heard the expression that what goes around comes back around. Normally when someone uses this cliché, it's because a person has done something negative in his past that is now coming back to haunt him later in life. I was in a grocery store a few months ago when I overheard a man next to me relate a story about someone he knew who was going through a difficult time. The person telling the story explained that he was sure the person was struggling because of a sin that he had committed earlier in life. He even went so far as to quote Hosea 8:7a. *"For they have sown the wind, and they shall reap the whirlwind."* It's true that the principle of sowing and reaping is Biblically founded, but I think sometimes people tend to focus on only the negative connotation of this teaching. Quite often it seems to be missed that if you do good things in life, good will come back around to you as well.

> *"Be not deceived; God is not mocked: for whatsoever a man soweth, that shall he also reap. [8]For he that soweth to his flesh shall of the flesh reap corruption; but he that soweth to the Spirit shall of the Spirit reap life everlasting. [9]And let us not be weary in well doing: for in due season we shall reap, if we faint not. [10]As we have therefore opportunity, let us do good unto all men, especially unto them who are of the household of faith."* (Galatians 6:7-10)

These verses teach that if we sow to the Spirit, we will reap of the Spirit as well! So what should we do with this information? *"As we have therefore opportunity, let us do good unto all men."* And don't worry if it takes a while for things to come back to you. The Bible promises that *"...in due season we shall reap, if we faint not."*

It is our responsibility as Christians to use the lessons, experiences, and pain that God has given to us in order to make a difference in the lives of others. Whether it is encouraging them, inspiring them, or comforting them, we have to make ourselves available to God to be used as He will.

> *"Finally, be ye all of one mind, **having compassion one of another, love as brethren, be pitiful, be courteous**: [9]Not rendering evil for evil, or railing for railing: but contrariwise blessing; knowing that ye are thereunto called, that ye should inherit a blessing. [10]For he that will love life, and see good days, let him refrain his tongue from evil, and his lips that they speak no guile."* (I Peter 3:8-10)

A Man Who did everything that has been addressed in this chapter once walked this earth. His entire life was based on the principle of helping the weak, and the Scripture gives record of His works. *"How God anointed Jesus of Nazareth with the Holy Ghost and with power: **who went about doing good**, and healing all that were oppressed of the devil; for God was with him."* (Acts 10:38) Could someone look at your life and say, he *"went about doing good"*? God has given you the opportunity to invest in other people's lives through the suffering that you have endured. Are you using and taking advantage of your God-given difficulty? I pray you are.

Make a Difference

Several years ago I heard a quote that revolutionized my life. The quotation is simple: "When I die...I want someone to thank God that I lived." It's simple. It's short. It's life-changing. I haven't always been successful in the endeavor, but ever since God brought this quote into my life, I have attempted to live in such a way that this expression could be said about me someday. One day when God calls me to Heaven, I pray that I will have lived in such a way that someone will be glad that I was here. Hopefully, someone will be glad that he knew me. Prayerfully, there will be someone who will say, "David...made a difference." *"And of some have compassion, making a difference."* (Jude 1:22)

*"...God hath made me to laugh,
so that all that hear will laugh with me."*

–Genesis 21:6

CHAPTER ELEVEN

A GREAT DOOR

Embracing the Opportunities of Difficulty

I remember the coach of the local speech and debate club leaning out of her car window saying, "We'll see you at club next Monday, right?" I smiled politely and said that I'd talk to my parents about it. That's what came out of my mouth, but what went through my head was, "Not a chance." I had absolutely no intention of showing up to a club devoted exclusively to public speaking and competitive debating. There were a few things that I thought I might be good at in life, but public speaking wasn't really high on that list. Remember those tumors that wreaked havoc on my oral cavity when I was younger? All of that was coursing through my mind as I listened to the debate coach trying to convince me that I should join the club.

The truth is that she didn't want me to join because she thought I was super-talented and would be successful in competitive speech and debate. That wasn't the case at all. She only wanted me to come because one of the other kids had dropped out, and she desperately needed an even number of students to make all of the debate partnerships work. As much as I could potentially sympathize with her need for another body, I didn't think I was going to be a good fit for her at all given my medical history and speech problems.

Just to recap, the tumors that afflicted my body when I was younger left quite a significant amount of damage to my mouth. Most of my top teeth had been destroyed, and there was a large hole (cleft palate) in the top of my mouth. Part of my cheek bone had been destroyed as well, and most of the structure of my mouth had been distorted. It wasn't a secret that verbal communication wasn't going to come easy for me at all. In fact, for several years I went to speech therapy twice a week trying to learn how to speak. After years of therapy and exercises, I finally got to the point where most people could understand what I was saying, but even to this day, certain sounds and letter combinations are unclear and garbled. I still find that "s," "sp," and "sw" sounds are very difficult for me to make clear.

Due to all of my background with struggling to be able to speak effectively, I really didn't see public speaking in my future. If there was ever an area that God wanted to use me, this couldn't be it. I kept my promise to the coach though, and I went home and talked to my parents. Much to my surprise and astonishment, my parents thought I should give it a shot. Really!? Apparently, they had forgotten everything that had occurred in the last 16 years. Yes, I had done some public speaking classes before, but that was all basic stuff. It wasn't competitive speaking where I would be against thousands of teenagers who seemingly all wanted to be lawyers or politicians. My mom and dad convinced me to go to that first club meeting though. I think they knew something that I didn't. But there is one thing I'm sure of—God definitely knew something that none of us did.

That was the fall semester of 2006. Throughout the first semester, we worked on basic speaking and argumentation. I had a good time and enjoyed what I was learning, but again, I really hadn't had to do much speaking yet, so I wasn't that concerned. I went ahead and joined the club full-time and started working toward preparing for the competition season that would begin in the spring semester. The league of which I was now a part is the third largest high school speech and debate organization in America, and there are literally thousands of young people from across the country against whom I was soon to be competing. I really had never thought about the national competitions because I did not think there was any chance at all that I would be good enough to advance to that level.

In December of 2006, my debate club traveled to Birmingham, Alabama, for a practice tournament. I didn't know anybody as I walked into the church where the event was being held, but I was immediately struck by a feeling of not belonging. It wasn't because anyone was impolite or unkind to me; it was just because all of the kids were so talented and polished. They were fluent and impressive speakers who looked the part with their suits, ties, and black briefcases. I certainly wasn't expecting the event to go well for me. But most of all, in the back of my mind were the lingering concerns about how intelligible my own speaking would be. I did not tell anyone about how worried I was, but I was indeed very nervous about how well I would be able to be understood—especially while competing against people who sounded like the Great Communicator, Ronald Reagan.

The way that the practice tournament worked was that we had four debate rounds against randomly selected teams. My debate partner and I did our best and enjoyed ourselves during those rounds, but of course we weren't sure how well we had done because the judge's decisions were announced after the last round was over for the day. That was when everyone was truly taken aback because my partner and I had won every single round. We were 4-0! I couldn't believe it. Actually, nobody could believe it. Everyone was surprised that a first-year debate team was able to put together an undefeated record at their first ever tournament.

A couple of weeks later, we went to the first official tournament of the year for our region. It was a two-day event held at a church just a couple of miles from my house. Again the Lord blessed, and my partner and I finished in seventh place overall. But what again surprised everyone was when the tournament director announced the individual speaker awards during the ceremony at the end of the tournament. During the preliminary rounds of the tournament, all of the judges gave the individual speakers points based upon their performance. A speaker could get anywhere between 6 and 30 points in a round. These points were then tabulated, and the speakers who accumulated the highest point total won individual speaker awards.

I had accrued enough points to finish in second place in individual speaker points! I was stunned! Out of all of the amazing speakers at that tournament, I had been ranked the second best? That wasn't what I was expecting at all. Now of course, because you are dealing with human judges, just because I received the second highest point total didn't necessarily mean that I was actually the second best speaker in our region, but it was still a significant step for a kid who had the medical history I did.

The year went on, and things continued to go well—better than I ever expected. Debate went fairly well with the highlight of the year being a tournament where my partner and I advanced all the way to the final round and finished in second place overall. In that last round, we debated in front of an audience of close to 200 people, competed against two former national champions, and were judged by an Alabama Supreme Court Justice. We lost that round, but our second place finish was still an unexpected and exciting accomplishment.

However, it was not in debate, but in the individual speaking events that I really began to excel. I competed in three individual events that first year. During the various preliminary tournaments in our region, I managed to qualify in all of them for the regional invitational tournament held at the end of the year. At that tournament I qualified for the national championship tournament in all three of my individual events plus debate. A couple of months earlier, I had been reluctant to begin public speaking at all, and now I was preparing to travel to Belton, Texas, to compete against the best high school speakers in the country. I cannot adequately express how amazed I was at the goodness of God as He continued to take me places with my public speaking that I never dreamed possible because of my medical history.

My expectations going into the national championship tournament were basically non-existent. I was so happy and thankful just to be there that I was not anticipating doing well from a competitive standpoint at all. Again, however, God intended for that to be a week that I would never forget. I advanced to the semi-final round in all three of my individual speaking events and went to finals in one of them. The speech that I took to the final round was a ten-minute piece that I had written. The final round went well, but I really wasn't expecting to place very high. I had made it all the way to the final eight speakers in the nation. At that point, I didn't much care where I finished. I felt so blessed already that I could have finished dead last in that final round, and I would have still been thrilled with the tournament. At the awards ceremony, the league president began calling out the placings for the event in which I had advanced to the finals. He read off the names of the eight, seventh, sixth, fifth, and fourth place finishers. He had not yet called my name, and I remember thinking how cool it was going to be to finish third. Then the moderator called out the third place finisher's name, and it wasn't mine! It was down to two. Second place wasn't my name either.

I won! In my first year, I was a national champion. I really couldn't believe it. As I walked across the platform to receive the first place trophy, all I could think about was how God was using a kid with such an unlikely background to accomplish things that nobody thought possible. But He wasn't done making dreams come true....

I still had another year of eligibility in the organization in which I had competed. That summer as I prepared to compete for another year, God worked miraculously in several areas. First of all, this was the summer that I had the major reconstructive surgery on my mouth. Nobody really knew how that operation would affect my speaking ability, but God allowed me to recuperate relatively quickly and get back to speaking within a few months of the surgery. He also worked out some details that allowed me to join a speech and debate club about two hours from my house. Every Friday I would drive to my new club where I was trained by some of the best speech and debate coaches in the country. God also blessed me with an absolutely tremendous debate partner who was extremely talented but also just a great guy who kept the year fun and exciting.

The competition season started again in January of 2008, and things immediately began to go well. My partner and I won two tournaments during the qualifying segment of the year and qualified to go back to the national championship tournament for the second consecutive year. Again though, it was in my individual speaking events that the Lord really blessed.

The league in which I competed had an award called the Individual Events Sweepstakes Award. At every tournament this award was given to the speaker who did the best overall in the various individual events. Going into the national championship tournament in the summer of

2008, I had won the sweepstakes award at five out of the six tournaments that I had attended. I also qualified in the maximum number of individual events (5) to compete with at nationals. Several people mentioned to me before the tournament that I might have a chance to win first place sweepstakes at the national championship, but I never even allowed myself to think about that possibility. By this point, trust me, I knew God was capable of doing anything He wanted, but I just didn't have enough confidence in myself that I could win an award that was indicative of being the best overall speaker in the nation.

The events leading up to the June national championship were truly miraculous in several different ways. My eye problems began to really become significant, and there were times when nobody was sure whether or not I would be able to compete. That was a little bit scary. I had spent all year preparing for this one-week tournament, and I had doctors telling me that they didn't think I should go. Three days before the regional invitational tournament, my retina detached for the first time. The doctor's immediate reaction was to inform me that I would have to miss the tournament. I was crushed. How was I going to break the news to my debate partner? If I didn't go to this tournament, then there was a chance that we wouldn't receive one of our region's limited number of slots to the national tournament.

My retina had detached on a Saturday, so Monday morning was the first chance that I could have the surgery to repair the damage. I had the operation Monday morning and then came to see my doctor the next morning in his office to see if things had gone well enough for him to let me go to the tournament. I could hardly believe it when the doctor smiled and said, "Good luck at your tournament this week, David." Tuesday afternoon my family loaded up our van and drove to Monroe, Louisiana, for the regional tournament.

I was so thankful to be at the tournament, but I have to admit that it was one of the most miserable experiences of my life. "Horrible" just really doesn't seem to adequately describe how I felt as I tried to compete. I was wearing a large patch over my right eye because it was bloodshot red, and I didn't want anyone to have to see it while I was speaking, but the truth was that the eye was very inflamed and painful. Furthermore, the eye absolutely would not stop watering. It was like I had a miniature waterfall located on my face! Let's just say it was a little bit distracting trying to give a speech in front of an audience while water is literally dripping down your chin. I also had to deal with the problems caused by all of the medication that I was taking.

The tournament began on Wednesday, and quite honestly I was still feeling affected by the anesthesia from the surgery. Even after the anesthesia finally wore off, I was still taking massive amounts of prescribed painkillers and steroids. It was incredibly difficult to focus and stay poised as the room spun around me every time I stood up. It wasn't easy, but I think the entire tournament was summed up well by a close friend of mine.

I was sitting in the corner of a room with my head in my hands during one of the breaks at the tournament. Normally during an intermission in the competition, I would have been socializing and talking with my friends, but because I felt so awful, I just wanted some peace and quiet when I could get it. I'm not sure how long I sat there by myself, but after quite a while when I finally looked up, a wonderful friend of mine was sitting next to me. I don't know how long she had been sitting there or why she didn't say anything, but for some reason just knowing that she cared enough to sit by me when she knew I was in pain made all the difference. But before I could say anything, she smiled and said, "Dave, I don't know why God has given you this difficulty right now during the most important part of the competition season, but I think it's because He wants to do something amazing." She was right. He did.

Despite the circumstances, God blessed me at the regional tournament as well. I won overall sweepstakes again, and as I said before, I qualified in all of my events to the national championship tournament. It was awe-inspiring to see God work through all of the pain and trials of that week. There were five weeks between the regional and national tournaments. The first four weeks went very well with the continued recovery of the eye, and it appeared that I was going to be fine to compete at nationals. Well, it wasn't going to be quite that simple, but then again... what miracles are?

I woke up exactly one week before national competition was to begin and immediately knew something was wrong with my eye. The pressure in the eye had plummeted, and my vision was completely gone again. Later that day my doctor confirmed what I already knew to be truth. The retina had detached again. The previous surgery had been unsuccessful. There were again some fairly tense moments as I waited to find out if I would be medically cleared to compete at the most important tournament of the year. I am somewhat embarrassed to admit this, but I probably prayed more desperately that afternoon at the doctor's office than I have at any other point in my life. Thank God for answered prayers though! The doctor said that my eye was very fragile, but he thought with large doses of medication, the situation could probably be stabilized until after the tournament. I was so relieved. God had come through for me again!

The national championship was sort of a blur. It just seemed to go by so quickly that I barely had time to realize what was happening. The first three days were filled with preliminary rounds that just seemed to go "okay." I wasn't that excited about how I was doing, but I did not think I was doing poorly either. I knew I wasn't completely focused because my eye was such a distraction, but the Lord really gave me the strength to block out the medical situation long enough for me to give every speech everything that I had. After the preliminary rounds had concluded, a banquet was held, and all of the competitors found out who had advanced and whose season had come to an end. I was stunned as I learned that I had advanced in every single one of my events. That was the first time that it ever entered my mind that I had the opportunity to win sweepstakes.

There was still work to be done. I competed in all five of my individual events in the semi-final round, but only three of my events advanced to the final round. Other competitors took three events to the final round as well, so at that point I wasn't feeling nearly as good about my chance to win. All of the speeches in the final round went well however, and all I could do was wait for the results to be announced at the awards ceremony later in the day.

I'm not the kind of person who gets nervous very easily. This time was an exception. I was pretty much miserable as the hours ticked by toward the awards ceremony. When the ceremony finally did begin, it was as if my body kicked into overdrive on excitement. I was not doing a very good job sitting still while the tournament administration made announcements and thanked everyone who had helped to make the event possible. The ceremony was exciting for me because several of my friends did very well and because my debate partner and I finished in twelfth place overall. Both of us were very satisfied with finishing twelfth in the nation. But for me anyway, everything was just building toward the Individual Event Sweepstakes Award. The league president went through all ten individual speaking events and then all of the debate awards. The ceremony seemingly lasted for hours. All of my events were going well though. In the three events that I took to finals, I finished first, second, and fifth respectively. I knew with those finishes, there was still a chance that I could win first place overall. That thought didn't change how anxious I was though.

The very last part of the awards ceremony was of course the sweepstakes award. The announcer started at twenty-fourth place and began ranking the top speakers in the country. Again it seemed to last forever. Several of my friends gathered around me, and you could literally feel the tension of the moment. They all knew what could happen, and they knew what it would mean. They knew my history. They knew that by all reasonable medical standards, I shouldn't have been there. But they also knew the God Who had already taken me so much further than anyone could have ever expected. Names continued to be called out until there were just two places left to be announced. Second place wasn't me.

In spite of how exhausted I was physically, I distinctly remember the surge of energy that flooded through my body as the announcement was made: "First place individual events sweepstakes champion…(yes…it was really this long of a pause)…David McCroskey." I stood up and was instantly inundated by greetings from my friends who were probably more excited than I was. As I made my way through the crowd, I passed my parents. They were both crying. They understood. It was just as much a victory for them as it was for me. They knew what God had just done. He had just brought me from a speech therapy patient to a national speech champion.

Why do I share that rather lengthy story with you? I assure you it's not to brag. It is certainly not because I want you to think that I'm somebody special. It's because I want you to see that God gave me an opportunity, and He used it to help me and many others around me as well. When He first presented the door of competitive speech and debate before me, I didn't think it was for me. Had God forgotten my medical history? Had it slipped His mind that I had always struggled to communicate verbally? Public speaking was one of the last avenues that I had any business attempting. I was hesitant. I was reluctant. I almost said no. I almost rejected the magnificent opportunity to bring honor, glory, and praise to His name. I almost didn't walk through the door. Thank God I did.

My experiences in speech and debate have truly opened my eyes to the power and might of our Lord. When we are weak, He truly is strong. He really does know how to take a difficulty in our life and use it for our best and His much-deserved honor. But here is the part that I don't want you to miss. I wouldn't have the story that I just told you if I had not embraced the opportunity that God presented. By faith, I had to step out of my comfort zone and let Him handle the rest. I had to trust that He had a plan and that He was going to take my weaknesses and use them to do something unexpected and inexplicable.

Later a lady who was at the awards ceremony at nationals told me something that I did not know. Of course I knew that when I won, the entire audience gave me a standing ovation, but she told me that every person in the room who knew me personally was in tears as I received my award. She talked to me about how everyone was so inspired by what had just happened—not because of me, but because of what God had just done through me. God had just told everyone in that room who knew me, "You can make it, too. You have trials and troubles as well, and you can accomplish things that you don't think you're capable of… just like David."

To me, that's what matters. The trophy doesn't matter. The recognition doesn't matter. It's all about anyone who might have been encouraged and uplifted because I was willing to walk through the great door that God had given me. I have no doubt that all of the other extremely talented speakers in the organization through which I participated will go on to accomplish great things. There will be dazzling politicians, skilled lawyers, and influential businessmen that come out of the class of competitors of which I was a member. Many of the students have gone on to Ivy League schools, lucrative scholarships, and incandescently bright futures. But that's not for me. That's not what it's about from my perspective. All of my participation during the past two years in competitive speech and debate has been for the one person who feels a little bit stronger and a little bit more hopeful about the circumstances of his life. That's why I'm glad I walked through the door.

God is going to present a door before you as well. He has a plan for the difficulties and challenges that He has brought into your life as well. He will give you an opportunity that at first will scare you. Your immediate reaction will probably be, "I can't do that." But you must! You must embrace the opportunity. You must walk through the door. For your sake, yes, but for the people that are watching you as well. They need you to be strong. They need you to use your difficulty in a way that makes you feel vulnerable. They need you to sacrifice. They need you to do what you don't think you can…or even should try.

The Bible gives a parable that is very applicable for this topic.

"For the kingdom of heaven is as a man travelling into a far country, who called his own servants, and delivered unto them his goods. [15]And unto one he gave five talents, to another two, and to another one; to every man according to his several ability; and straightway took his journey. [16]Then he that had received the five talents went and traded with the same, and made them other five talents. [17]And likewise he that had received two, he also gained other two. [18]But he that had received one went and digged in the earth, and hid his lord's money. [19]After a long time the lord of those servants cometh, and reckoneth with them. [20]And so he that had received five talents

came and brought other five talents, saying, Lord, thou deliveredst unto me five talents: behold, I have gained beside them five talents more. [21]His lord said unto him, Well done, thou good and faithful servant: thou hast been faithful over a few things, I will make thee ruler over many things: enter thou into the joy of thy lord. [22]He also that had received two talents came and said, Lord, thou deliveredst unto me two talents: behold, I have gained two other talents beside them. [23]His lord said unto him, Well done, good and faithful servant; thou hast been faithful over a few things, I will make thee ruler over many things: enter thou into the joy of thy lord. [24]Then he which had received the one talent came and said, Lord, I knew thee that thou art a hard man, reaping where thou hast not sown, and gathering where thou hast not strawed: [25]And I was afraid, and went and hid thy talent in the earth: lo, there thou hast that is thine. [26]His lord answered and said unto him, Thou wicked and slothful servant, thou knewest that I reap where I sowed not, and gather where I have not strawed: [27]Thou oughtest therefore to have put my money to the exchangers, and then at my coming I should have received mine own with usury. [28]Take therefore the talent from him, and give it unto him which hath ten talents. [29]For unto every one that hath shall be given, and he shall have abundance: but from him that hath not shall be taken away even that which he hath. [30]And cast ye the unprofitable servant into outer darkness: there shall be weeping and gnashing of teeth." (Matthew 25:14-30)

God has given you talents. God has given you skills, abilities, and gifts that you might not even recognize at the moment. What are these talents? They are your cup. What God wants to use in your life is that part of you that you probably consider the most unusable. But He isn't necessarily interested in doing what makes sense to the mind of finite man, but rather in using what will bring the most glory to Him. So here are the questions that you must answer:

- Are you going to bury your talent?
- In fear, are you going to cower away from the opportunities that He brings your way?

- Are you going to hide your talent?
- Or are you going to take a risk?
- Are you going to try something that doesn't make sense on paper?
- Are you going to use your difficulty in whatever way God asks you?
- Are you going to hear, "Well done, good and faithful servant"?

When you start using the difficulties of your life to do things for God and His children, that is when everything is really going to start making sense. That's when questions such as, "Why?" are going to start getting answered. That is when your cup will no longer seem like a burden but rather the blessing that God intended. We are all familiar with the tremendous struggles that Job endured in the Old Testament. Have you ever noticed when God delivered him from his oppressive situation? God changed everything about Job's situation when he used his experiences to help those around him.

> *"And the LORD **turned the captivity of Job, when he prayed for his friends:** also the LORD gave Job twice as much as he had before.* [11]*Then came there unto him all his brethren, and all his sisters, and all they that had been of his acquaintance before, and did eat bread with him in his house: and they bemoaned him, and comforted him over all the evil that the LORD had brought upon him: every man also gave him a piece of money, and every one an earring of gold.* [12]*So the LORD blessed the latter end of Job more than his beginning: for he had fourteen thousand sheep, and six thousand camels, and a thousand yoke of oxen, and a thousand she asses.* [13]*He had also seven sons and three daughters."*

(Job 42:10-13)

Because of everything that Job had gone through, he truly knew how to pray for his friends to be helped. And it was when Job used his pain and agony to cry out to God on behalf of his friends that everything changed. The verses go on to emphasize how amazingly God blessed Job after his trial had ended. Likewise, God has rich blessings in store for all of His children. But what's the step we have to take? We have to embrace the opportunities that He presents. It's not enough to just accept and embrace the difficulties of life. *"Even so faith, if it hath not works, is dead, being alone."* (James 2:17) It's dead. It's all worthless and useless until we accomplish that which God had in mind when He afflicted us in the first place. We must embrace and use our difficulty.

I can't tell you what door God wants you to walk through. Only you can know that. Maybe He wants you to start a foundation. Perhaps He wants you to teach a class. Maybe you need to write a book or tell your story. I don't know. But I think you do. And if you don't, then I'd encourage you to ask God to reveal to you what it is that He wants you to do. He'll show you. He has plans for your life. There's no doubt about that. All you need to worry about now is your own willingness to do what God calls you to do. Let God worry about opening the right door in His own timing. *"Furthermore, when I came to Troas to preach Christ's gospel, and a door was opened unto me of the Lord."* (II Corinthians 2:12) God will open the appropriate door at exactly the right time. You just have to walk through it—whether or not you think you can.

Let me finish this chapter by saying that I'm not promising that things are going to be easy. I know, I'm not seemingly ending on a happy note, right? Sorry, but it's the truth. *"For a great door and effectual is opened unto me, and there are many adversaries."* (I Corinthians 16:9) There are many adversaries. There will be bumps in the road. You may get lost a time or two. You may have a few retina problems that you never saw coming. But in the end, it's not going to matter. Because what lies on the other side of the door is worth everything it may take to walk across the threshold of the doorway. There is a great door. Walk through it. Never look back.

CHAPTER TWELVE

MORE THAN CONQUERORS

Putting It All Together

Wow! We're here. I confess that it is with a little bit of emotion that I write the final chapter to what has been quite a journey for me personally. I started writing this book because I felt like God wanted to share with more people what He had already taught me, but now I think that possibly it was for my benefit that He called me to begin this project. I've learned so much. I've grown. I've immersed myself in the Word of God and have come out more in awe of my Creator and Saviour than ever before. It is my sincere prayer that through the reading of this book, you have fallen deeper in love with Him as well. That's the key. Honestly, if you get nothing else out of what I have addressed, but you close the back cover of this book just a little bit more amazed by the great God that we serve, then I would consider every moment that I've spent entirely worth it.

If we truly love Christ, there is absolutely nothing that can hold us back. Tumors, arthritis, blindness, cancer, emotional scars, financial pressures, or whatever else it is that might afflict us cannot compete against the fire that is lit by a sincere and passionate love for Christ. *"But as it is written, Eye hath not seen, nor ear heard, neither have entered into the heart of man, the things which God hath prepared for them that love him."* (I Corinthians 2:9) I just want you to love Him more. That is my hope and prayer. I want you to do great things for Him prompted out of a desire and willingness to make your life count for eternity.

You know you have a cup. You know that your response to the difficulties that present themselves will make all the difference. Are you going to realize that what you consider your weakness or challenge is actually a gift from God? Remember not to waste time asking God "Why?" and instead spend all of your effort figuring out how your pain fits into what

God wants you to accomplish for His kingdom. Please let go of whatever bitterness or anger that might still be trying to grab a stronghold in your heart. It's not worth it. Those negative emotions are only going to drag you backward and plunge you into a state of useless depression.

Fall in love with the wonderful Father Who has given you a burden to bear because He wants to use you in a magnificent way. Be content with the situations that you cannot change. Live your life like there's no tomorrow. Embrace and be thankful for the pain that has made you who you are. Surrender to the masterful design that has been prepared for you by your God. Use your limitations to encourage, inspire, and motivate those around you. Smile. Brighten somebody's day. Sacrifice and invest in those around you who need your influence. Embrace the opportunities that God presents to you. Walk through the great and effectual door that is in your path. Accept, embrace, and use the difficulty that God has given you.

All of those steps must be taken in order for you to get the maximum amount of productivity and satisfaction out of your troubles and trials. Stopping halfway would ruin everything and severely limit God's plans. You cannot accomplish part one and then forget about parts two and three. You can't do part one and two but never surrender to three. You have to accept, embrace, and use. That's so critical. It's all about taking that next step. Don't be content being mediocre. Average is not okay. You aren't happy with just accepting. You aren't satisfied with merely embracing. You aren't content with just using. You're going to do all three. You're going to push the limits of productiveness. You are going to get everything out of your pain and difficulty that God has intended. You aren't going to hold anything back.

In this book I have attempted to use a lot of Scripture. Yes, a big part of this book has just been my heart and what God has taught me so far in my young life, but from the very beginning I have endeavored to build this book upon a solidly Biblical foundation. With that in mind, I sought to use as many Biblical examples and illustrations as possible, and the entire book is littered with verses. But I have resisted the urge to use one particular portion of Scripture during the writing of this book because I wanted to save it for the very end. Here it is now.

*"Who shall separate us from the love of Christ? shall tribula-
tion, or distress, or persecution, or famine, or nakedness, or peril,
or sword?* [36]*As it is written, For thy sake we are killed all the day
long; we are accounted as sheep for the slaughter.* [37]*Nay, in all
these things we are **more than conquerors** through him that loved
us.* [38]*For I am persuaded, that neither death, nor life, nor angels,
nor principalities, nor powers, nor things present, nor things to
come,* [39]*Nor height, nor depth, nor any other creature, shall be
able to separate us from the love of God, which is in Christ Jesus
our Lord."* (Romans 8:35-39)

This passage of Scripture sums up everything that I've tried to convey
in the writing of this book. Thus, it is why I chose, "More Than Conquerors" as the title for the last chapter of this book. That's what I want
you to be. That's what I want to be: more than a conqueror.

What is going to keep us from serving God and making a difference
in this world for Christ? Pain? Difficulty? Challenges? Persecution? Distresses? Tribulations? I don't think so. None of these things can stop us.
Why? Because you know what a conqueror does with a roadblock? He
overcomes it. He doesn't let it get in his way. He pushes forward. Listen,
you aren't just a conqueror. You are more than a conqueror. You are
somebody special who has been providentially prepared to do something
that cannot be explained except by the love and power of God. *"But ye
are a chosen generation, a royal priesthood, an holy nation, a peculiar people; that ye should shew forth the praises of him who hath called you out
of darkness into his marvellous light."* (I Peter 2:9)

You keep moving forward even when you don't have the strength.
How do you do it? You don't. God does. And He doesn't just take you
to the first step in the process and then abandon you. No, He takes you
all the way to victory. He makes you more than you could have ever become on your own. He makes you more than a conqueror though His
enduring love.

The world is going to look at your new outlook on adversity, and they
aren't going to get it. They won't understand. That's okay. Maybe you
can use your difficulty to help them see the blessing that is their cup as

well. But even if nobody ever comes around to your new perspective, that will be okay, too. This is personal anyway. It's about you and your relationship to the affliction that God has given you.

So go ahead. Change your attitude toward difficulty. It's a gift from God. Drink your cup. Love the life that He has given you. Make some memories as you explore the greatness of your Father. Laugh. Smile. Dry your eyes and push forward. Fall in love with God and let Him show you great and mighty things.

Oh, and your pain? Your difficulty? Your cup?

Accept it.

Embrace it.

Use it.

May God make us all more than conquerors...and may you live every day like it's *The Best Day of Your Life*!